The 27th Mile

Going the Extra Mile to Support the Victims of the Boston Marathon Bombing

edited by
Ray Charbonneau

ISBN-13: 978-1490376295
ISBN-10: 1490376291

More info:
http://www.the27thmile.com
the27thmile@y42k.com

Book design: Y42K Book Production Services
http://www.y42k.com/bookproduction.html

Cover design: Ryan Bradley
http://cargocollective.com/ryanwbradley

Dedication

The 27th Mile is dedicated to the memory of:

> Martin Richard
> Krystle Campbell
> Lu Lingzi
> Sean Collier

and to everyone injured on Boylston Street at the 2013 Boston Marathon.

Contents

Dedication 3

Write on Hereford, Left on Boylston 9

An Open Letter from Past Boston Champions 11
   Contributed by Amby Burfoot

So I Went for a Run 13
   by Mark Remy

Running Revolution 15
   by Jeff Galloway

It's a Miracle 23
   by Lawrence Block

Monkeys and Bonobos 33
   by Jesse Parent

Essential Lydiard 35
   by Lorraine Moller

All You Need Is a Thumb 45
   by Chris Cooper

Running with Buddy 49
   by Chris Russell

The Long Haul 53
   by Ben Tanzer

All the Way to San Francisco 59
   by Willy Palomo

Vanishing Act 61
   by Julie Greicius

Running Home 69
    by Amby Burfoot
Something to Run For 73
    by Ray Sespaniak
The Runner 89
    by Ben Tanzer
Baby Birds 95
    by Willy Palomo
We Who Watch 97
    by Joe Henderson
Rejoice! We Conquer! 105
    by Cristina Negrón
Joggling Red Rock Canyon 121
    by Perry Romanowski
I Had to Pee 127
    by Lawrence Block
Rage, Rage 131
    by Jason Fisk
On the Run from Dogs and People 137
    by Hal Higdon
I Don't Run Boston 153
    by Caryl Haddock
Shared Vision 157
    by Ray Charbonneau

Do We Need an Ambulance for Cross Country? 169
    by Grace Butcher
Awakenings and Resolutions 173
    by Kathrine Switzer
Finding Resilience in the Forest..181
    by Vanessa Runs
Wheels 185
    by RJ Walker
Why I'll Run the Marathon in 2014 189
    by Ray Charbonneau
Acknowledgements...193

Write on Hereford, Left on Boylston

The Boston Marathon occupies a unique position in the world of running. The race is a monument, created over 117 years from the struggles of hundreds of thousands of runners attempting to celebrate the spirit of Pheidippides with a victory over the distance. The foundation of that monument is the love and support from the millions more who have cheered the runners on their way.

In 2013, that edifice was attacked.

Johnny Kelley must have been shocked when he heard the thunder, looked down from above, and saw smoke rising from near the finish line he crossed fifty-eight times on Patriots Days past.

One thing is always present after any tragedy: the powerful human need to help. First responders rushing towards the blast as others ran away, runners tearing IVs from their arms in the medical tent to make room for those with greater needs, Boston area residents interrupting their lives to abet police officers as they tracked down the perpetrators.

We're a group of writers who run and friends who wanted, in some small way, to be part of that effort. We got together to create the book you hold in your hands. It is dedicated to everyone who loves running or runners—first and foremost to those who were killed or injured, but to the rest of us, too. In particular, the book is dedicated to the people who, even as they eat dinner with their family, put in another eight hours at work, or sit and read this book, have already planned when they'll go out for their next run.

Within this book, you'll find stories about and reflections upon the events of Marathon Monday 2013. Many good things happened on April 15, mostly in spite of the bombing, but sometimes because of it. We want to remember those while we mourn the people who were lost and feel sorrow for those who were injured.

You'll also find pieces that extol the spirit that first got us out on the roads to run, that brought us to Boston on a sunny spring day, and that will bring us back to Hopkinton next year, and in the years that follow. This is the spirit we celebrate every time we go for a run, whatever the distance. Thanks for celebrating with us.

All proceeds from sales of The 27th Mile *will go to support the victims of the tragedy on Boylston St. Please tell your friends about this book. For more info, visit our web site at www.the27thmile.com, or contact us at the27thmile@y42k.com.*

An Open Letter from Past Boston Champions

Contributed by Amby Burfoot

We, the undersigned Boston Marathon champions, wish to offer our deepest sympathies to the individuals and families harmed by Monday's tragic bomb explosions.

At the same time, we express our appreciation to the citizens of Boston, who have embraced us for so many years, and we likewise declare our support for all future Boston Marathons. We shall return.

Some of us will toe the starting line again next April, even though we had no such intention before Monday's events. Others will return to swell the sideline and sidewalk crowds more fully than ever before. All of us, even if not present in person, will be there in spirit.

The Boston Marathon has long been known for its start in rural Hopkinton, its screeching coeds at Wellesley College, and its leg-searing Heartbreak Hill. These, however, are mere geographies. To us, the essence of Boston has always been its huge, supportive crowds—the biggest, loudest, and most knowledgeable in the running world.

Those killed and wounded on Monday had gathered at the finish-line area with a single purpose: to cheer for Boston marathoners. That makes them part of our extended family. When they cheer for one Boston runner, they cheer for all of us.

We will never forget this year's victims or the millions like them who line the Hopkinton-to-Boston streets each April, challenging us to be our best. Without them, we could not run so strong or reach our goals.

We know they will be back next April in greater numbers than ever and more enthusiastic than ever. They are resilient,

11

they are defiant, and they are enduring. So are we.

We agree with President Obama, who said in Boston: "Next year, on the third Monday in April, the world will return to this great American city to run harder than ever, and to cheer even louder, for the 118th Boston Marathon. Bet on it."

We're betting on it. We shall return.

Sincerely,
Gayle Barron: 1978
Sara Mae Berman: 1969, 1970, 1971
Amby Burfoot: 1968
Jack Fultz: 1976
Roberta Gibb: 1966, 1967, 1968
Jacqueline Hansen: 1973
Ron Hill: 1970
Nina Kuscsik: 1972
Greg Meyer: 1983
Lorraine Moller: 1984
Uta Pippig: 1994, 1995, 1996
Lisa Weidenbach Rainsberger: 1985
Bill Rodgers: 1975, 1978, 1979, 1980
Allison Roe: 1981
Alberto Salazar: 1982
Joan Benoit Samuelson: 1979, 1983

This piece previously appeared on multiple running-related web sites.

So I Went for a Run

by Mark Remy

I was angry, so I went for a run. And things got better.

I was confused, so I went for a run. And things got better.

I was exhausted, so I went for a run. And things got better.

I was lost, unsure, empty, afraid. Certain that whatever was left of my sanity had snapped, had come untethered and floated away, to a place so high and remote that I would never see it again, and that even if I did, I wouldn't recognize it.

So I went for a run. And things got better.

I felt like things could not possibly get worse, so I went for a run. And things got better.

(Another time, I felt like things could not get much better. I went for a run. Things got much better.)

After enough miles, over enough runs and enough years, I realized: No matter what, no matter when, or where, or why, I can find my shoes and go for a run and things will get better.

And that realization? Just knowing that?

It made things better.

Mark Remy is an editor at large for Runner's World *and a veteran of 22 marathons, including six Boston Marathons. He writes* the popular *Remy's World* column on *RunnersWorld.com* and is the author of three books, including The Runner's Rule Book. *He lives in eastern Pennsylvania with his wife and two children. For more, visit markremy.com. "So I Went for a Run" originally appeared on runnersworld.com.*

Running Revolution

by Jeff Galloway

I was running before it caught on in America. Then in the late 60s I began to see a trickle of other runners out on the roads I once ran alone. By the early 70s, there were more, and now, millions are out running regularly. It seemed to have been a natural evolution, but in retrospect I can pinpoint a few key people who helped propel running into the revolution we now see in our towns and cities: three teachers — Arthur Lydiard, Bill Bowerman and Dr. Kenneth Cooper; and three runners — Amby Burfoot, Frank Shorter and Bill Rodgers. There were many others of course, but these six were catalysts, reflecting and magnifying the spirit of the times. They were at the right places, at the right time, with the right inspiration for the new outlook that was crucial to the birth of fitness running.

Running in New Zealand

In the 1940s, Arthur Lydiard, a former rugby player, overweight and working on the line at a New Zealand shoe factory, decided he had to make a change in his own life. Playing rugby on weekends had done nothing to deflate the spare tire around his middle, so he decided he'd try to run off the excess weight. But watching the local runners of the day was discouraging. They sped around and around the track at full speed until they collapsed. "No pain, no gain" was the philosophy of the day.

Arthur wanted to get in shape, but not that way. Instead, he took to the open New Zealand roads and embarked on a conditioning program of long, slow runs. Over the months he lost weight. Over the years he became addicted to running and discovered a long-hidden competitive spirit. He began to wonder how he might fare in a marathon and soon Lydiard the jogger became Lydiard the racer. He eventually came to represent New Zealand in the 1951 Commonwealth Games. A few local youngsters had begun running with Lydiard and eventually they asked if he'd be their coach. Lydiard agreed and developed his own program, emphasizing long slow runs, into a sequence of running workouts for his students. In the 1960 Rome Olympics, three of these neighborhood kids — Peter Snell, Murray Halberg and Barry Magee — won distance running medals. Lydiard became an acclaimed public figure and a national hero.

You might say Lydiard invented jogging. After the Olympics, he was frequently invited to speak to groups of sedentary men and women in their 30s, 40s and beyond. The people he talked to began to sense that they, like the formerly overweight rugby player, could run gently and improve their physical condition. Running not only could take off the weight but could be fun. Lydiard transformed the public's image of running from an intense, tedious, painful activity into a social, civilized component of the active New Zealand lifestyle. The credibility of the Olympic medals gave Lydiard a platform from which to reach millions. He got them out of their chairs and onto the roads in the early 60s, and the underground running movement began.

Jogging in America

Bill Bowerman is one of the most successful track coaches in the United States, but his role in bringing jogging to America is of even greater importance. In the winter of 1962, shortly after his University of Oregon four-mile relay team broke the world record, an invitation came for a match race with the team from New Zealand, the previous world record holders. Bowerman and his team were the guests of Arthur Lydiard.

"The first Sunday I was down there," Bowerman recalled in Bill Dellenger's book, *The Running Experience*, "Lydiard asked me if I wanted to go out for a run with a local jogging club. I was used to going out and walking 55 yards, jogging 55 yards, going about a quarter of a mile and figuring I had done quite a bit … . We went out and met a couple hundred people in a park — men, women, children, all ages and sizes. I was still full of breakfast as Lydiard pointed toward a hill in the distance and said we were going to run to Two Pine Knoll. It looked about 1 ½ miles away. We took off and I wasn't too bad for about ½ mile, and then we started up this hill. God, the only thing that kept me alive was the hope that I'd die. I moved right to the back of the group and an old fellow, I suppose he was around 70 years old, moved back with me and said, 'I see you're having trouble.' I didn't say anything — because I couldn't. So we took off down the hill and got back about the same time the people did who had covered the whole distance."

Bowerman, then 50, spent six weeks in New Zealand and ran every day. He lost nearly ten pounds and reduced his waistline by four inches. By the time he returned to Oregon, he had learned to jog — slowly and comfortably. As soon as he arrived home, he got a call from Jerry Uhrhammer, a sportswriter from the Eugene Register Guard. Uhrhammer wanted to know how the team had run, but Bowerman was much more excited about what he'd learned about jogging. Uhrhammer, who later became a jogger after open-heart surgery, published several articles based on Bowerman's revelations. Bowerman began staging Sunday morning runs and Uhrhammer publicized them.

Interest in the Sunday runs grew and Bowerman was asked to hold classes and clinics for neighborhood groups in Eugene. He did so, using some of his great Oregon distance runners as instructors. Before long Bowerman was overwhelmed with requests for information on this new phenomenon, so in 1966 he wrote a 20-page pamphlet — *Jogging* — with a Eugene cardiologist, Dr. Waldo Harris. The following year he published an expanded version of *Jogging*, which eventually sold over a million copies. The seeds of the jogging movement had been firmly planted in American soil.

Aerobics for Fitness

By 1960, more Americans were dying of heart disease than any other malady. A generation of Americans had leaped too quickly into the "good life."

People worked relatively hard until the mid-1940s. Finances kept meat consumption down and vegetable consumption up. Postwar prosperity, however, ushered in more leisure time, sedentary jobs and the funds to buy meat, cream, butter ... . The rate of heart disease climbed rapidly.

The Air Force became concerned when its pilots started dying of heart failure, often bringing multi-million dollar planes down with them. Air Force officials showed great interest when one of its young doctors, Kenneth Cooper, suggested a study to see if exercise could influence the risk factor in heart disease.

Cooper had been doing his medical residency in Boston when Bill Bowerman returned from New Zealand. A high school and college track star (he ran a 4:18 mile), Cooper had high blood pressure and had gained 40 pounds after medical school and internship. One day, as he recalls in *The Aerobics Program for Total Well-Being*, he decided to go water skiing. Having been an expert skier in his youth, he "... put on a slalom ski, told the driver to accelerate immediately to almost 30 miles per hour, and prepared to have a great time, just like in the old days.

"But I was in for a surprise.

"Within three to four minutes I was totally exhausted, and

I suddenly began to feel nauseated and weak. I told the boat driver to stop and get me back to land as quickly as possible. For the next 30 minutes, as I lay in nauseous agony on the shore, my head was spinning — and I honestly couldn't put a series of logical thoughts together."

This experience had the same effect on Cooper that the Sunday New Zealand run had on Bill Bowerman. He embarked upon an exercise and diet program that brought his weight down from 210 to 170 and reduced his body fat from 30% to 14%. His enthusiasm about exercise and the heart disease factor in airplane crashes convinced the Air Force brass of the value of his proposed testing program. The results of his studies were published in the landmark book *Aerobics*.

Cooper's book was a popular explanation of the facts that were beginning to pile up — that the good life would be cut short by poor eating habits, and that exercise could overcome many of the risk factors. Americans were receptive to these ideas. What good were a fine home, family and income without the good health to enjoy them?

Cooper's aim was to counteract the great lethargy and inactivity of most Americans by demonstrating the benefits of regular exercise. Most importantly, he showed how to do it. His point system gave even out-of-shape beginners a guide to exercise. Millions of today's fit Americans owe their good health to *Aerobics*.

The Final Push for Runners

Just as the Olympic medals provided the fuel for Lydiard's fitness wildfire in New Zealand, Olympic success by Americans showed fellow citizens that they, too, could be distance runners. Prior to the 1964 Tokyo Olympics, there had been only one gold medal won by an American distance runner since 1908 — Horace Ashenfelter in the 1952 steeplechase.

All this changed in the Tokyo Olympics when Billy Mills, a complete unknown, upset Australian star Ron Clark and Tunisian Mohamed Gammoudi to win the 10,000 meters. Four days later, American Bob Schul won the gold medal in the 5000 meters, and one second back in third place was Bill Dellenger, a 30-year-old high school track coach from Springfield, Oregon.

After years of small fields, the number of entries in major U.S. road races began to increase. In 1964 the Boston Marathon, the country's oldest road race, topped 300 entries for the first time. In 1967, it went to 479; in 1970, 1150. San Francisco's Bay to Breakers showed a similar growth. From a field of 15 in 1963, there were 124 the following year, 1241 in 1969 and 75,000 in 1984!

Although there were more racers each year, Americans had still not won the country's most important marathon — Boston — since 1957, when a schoolteacher from Groton, Connecticut named John J. Kelley broke the course record. After Kelley's victory, the Finns and Japanese dominated the event until 1968 when another New Englander, also from Groton and coached by Kelley, won. The now historic victory by my college roommate Amby Burfoot inspired thousands of recreational runners to take up the burgeoning sport.

Then, in the early 1970s, Frank Shorter, a Yale graduate and law student, developed into a national-class distance runner while a former track star in Oregon — Kenny Moore — moved off the track onto the roads and finished second in the 1970 Fukoka Marathon.

In 1971, both Shorter and Moore qualified for the Pan Am Games Marathon, which Shorter went on to win. Kenny Moore was a writer who went to work for *Sports Illustrated* where he wrote some inspiring accounts of world-class running that appealed to millions of readers.

The force of the American fitness revolution was

magnified in 1972 at the Munich Olympics by ABC Sports, which selected the marathon as one of their feature events. That Shorter beat one of the greatest fields ever assembled by more than two minutes was final confirmation that Americans could indeed be successful distance athletes.

Further proof was provided a few years later when Bill Rodgers surprised everyone by winning the 1975 Boston Marathon. He went on to win it in 1978, 1979 and 1980. The likeable Rodgers had a young-kid-like energy and openness so different from the cocky professional athletes of the day. He was accessible to the countless fans who lined up after the races to talk to him and he seldom refused an autograph

Just as Lydiard, Bowerman and Cooper were teachers who awakened an interest in the benefits of regular exercise, so Burfoot, Shorter and Rodgers (all from the "baby boom" generation) provided inspiration at key times to the country's growing group of runners. Americans knew that physical activity was the secret to their future health, and that running, for many, was the common denominator.

Jeff Galloway was an All-American collegiate athlete and a member of the 1972 US Olympic Team in the 10,000 meters. He remains a competitive athlete, with a successful masters running career. Galloway's quest for injury-free marathon training led him to develop a low mileage training program, the Galloway RUN-WALK method, which has a success rate of over 98%. For more, visit www.jeffgalloway.com. "Running Revolution" is an excerpt from Galloway's Book on Running.

It's a Miracle

by Lawrence Block

I'm sorry I can't remember learning to walk. Because it was a miracle. Oh, not a personal miracle—although, given my own innate clumsiness, it might well have been a marginally greater achievement for me than for the average incipient toddler. No, I've come to believe that learning to walk is a remarkable accomplishment for the entire human species, and not so much a miracle of evolution as a triumph of the will.

Nobody's born knowing how to do it. Grazing animals are on their feet and walking from the moment their mothers drop them; they have to be, or they won't keep up with the herd. But human infants are born as helpless as hamsters, and walking is something they have to learn. Or teach themselves, one might say. You can't read the manual, and, except by example, it's not something your parents can teach you. You crawl for a while, and then you stand up, and then you fall down. And you stand up and fall down again, and then the time comes when you stand up and take a few steps before falling down.

And so on.

And here's what makes it a miracle: Every child, but for the severely handicapped, does all this and does it successfully. Some are early walkers, some are late walkers. Some fall a little and some fall a lot. But, sooner or later, everybody walks. Nobody gets discouraged. Nobody gives up. Everybody stays with the program. And all this with no reward promised or punishment threatened, no hope of heaven or fear of hell, no carrot and no stick. Fall, rise, fall, rise, fall, rise—and walk.

Amazing.

23

Imagine, if you will, an adult in similar circumstances. Imagine the thoughts running through the adult mind:

The hell with this. What's the point in getting up when I'm only going to fall back down again? If I keep this up I'm only going to hurt myself. And look like all kinds of a damn fool while I'm at it.

What was so bad about crawling? I was pretty good at it. I got around just fine. Why would God give us hands and knees if he didn't expect us to get from place to place on them?

Who says everybody's meant to walk? It works for some people, but that doesn't mean it works for everybody. You need balance, for one thing, and you need good foot-eye coordination, and some of us aren't gifted in those departments.

I hate falling down. Makes me feel like a failure. Why reinforce that feeling by repeating the process?

It's hopeless.

What's the point, anyway? I mean, it's not as if there's anyplace I really have to get to. What's so bad about right here?

Screw it. If crawling's not good enough for them, they can pick me up and carry me. Because I've had it.

I quit.

But that never happens. I couldn't begin to guess what goes through a kid's mind when he's learning to walk, but I don't think the possibility of giving up ever enters into the equation. Sooner or later he learns. And, once he learns, he never forgets.

––––––––––

It was the spring of 1977, and I was living in a second-floor rear tenement apartment on Bleecker at Sullivan Street. I walked up Sullivan two blocks to Washington Square Park, stood on the sidewalk alongside the park facing east, and began to run. I proceeded counterclockwise around the little park. It's not microscopic, the circumference comes to just about five-eighths of a mile. (In other words, a kilometer, but I wasn't thinking in metric terms. Later, when I ran races measured in kilometers, the word would have more meaning to me.)

I couldn't run the whole way around. I ran as far as I could, until I had to walk and catch my breath. I walked until I felt I could run again, and ran until I had to walk again, and so on. I circled the park five times, which I figured came to three miles. Then I walked home, and took a shower that no one could have called premature.

I did this every morning.

My running wasn't much more than a shuffle, and I'm not sure I even called it running. I may have used the term "jogging," which was getting a lot of use at the time. I wouldn't use it now. There is, it seems to me, something both patronizing and trivializing about the term. If you're jogging, you're taking it easy. You're plugging away at it to keep in shape. It's good exercise, it'll help you keep your weight down, and if what they say is true, it'll work wonders for your cardiovascular system.

But it's not exactly athletic, is it? Dr. George Sheehan, a distinguished runner, writer, and physician, was once asked the difference between a jogger and a runner. "A race number," he replied.

Whatever it was, I did it every day. It wasn't like learning to ride a bike, or even like learning to walk in the first place, because there was no falling down involved. I ran until I had to walk, walked until I was able to run. The day came when I ran all the way around the park, a full five-eighths of a mile, before I had to walk. And there was another day, not too long afterward, when I was able to run for the whole three miles. Five laps, three miles, running all the way.

Who'd have thought it?

In a word, nobody.

For almost 39 years, if you saw me running, you knew I had a bus to catch—and that I'd probably miss it. I was born overweight and out of breath, and by the time I slimmed down some, I'd been smoking cigarettes for several years.

Back in seventh and eighth grades, they had a citywide running competition. At PS 66, the gym teacher, Mr. Geoghan, stood there with a stopwatch and had us run the length of the playground. He timed us in the 75-yard dash, and I wasn't the very slowest in my class, but I came close.

My freshman year in high school, my friend Ronnie Benice announced that he and another fellow, Ron Feldman, were going to try out for the cross-country team. I didn't even know what that was. "Come on along," he suggested. He explained what cross-country was, and I thought he was out of his mind. Run? Over hill and dale? Me? You're kidding, right? Both Rons ran cross-country in the fall and track in the spring. I spoke with Ron Feldman at a reunion a couple of years ago, and he said he still ran on a regular basis. Ron Benice is living in Florida, but I haven't been in touch with him in 25 years, so I have no idea if he's still running.

And then, 22 years after high school graduation, I was running around Washington Square Park. How the hell did that come to pass?

It was in 1959 that I was sent down from Antioch. (That's how the British would say it, and it sounds so much nicer than "expelled.") I'd spent the next 18 years getting married, siring daughters, writing books, moving around—back to Buffalo, out to Wisconsin, then to New Jersey. To say I drank my way into marriage isn't much of an exaggeration, and it's none at all to say I drank my way out of it. My first wife and I separated in 1973, and I moved to a studio apartment on West Fifty-Eighth Street. A year later, when I began chronicling the fictional adventures of Matthew Scudder, his hotel room was just around the block from me. How's that for coincidence?

He spent 20 years or so in that hotel room, but I was out of my apartment in two years. In 1977 I returned to New York, and I came very close to taking a room at Scudder's hotel, but instead I wound up signing a lease on that little apartment on Bleecker Street. I'd stopped smoking in September of 1974. I had stopped many times over the years, but this time it took. I never did go back to it. And, after several months on Bleecker Street, during which I put in some long hours at the Village Corner and the Kettle of Fish, I stopped drinking.

I'm sure that had a great deal to do with the running, although I never made the connection at the time. There couldn't have been more than a couple of weeks between my last drink and my first shuffling steps around the park, but when I was trying to work out the chronology the other day, I had trouble determining whether I was still drinking when I started running. Until then, I'd never thought of one thing as having led to the other.

But of course it did. All of a sudden I had all this nervous energy and nothing to do with it. I didn't think in those terms, not at all. I just had the thought one day, out of the blue, that I'd like to try running around the block. I didn't go to the park, just ran up Sullivan to West Third Street, turned left, went to MacDougal, turned left again ... and so on. Running for as long as I could, then gasping as I walked, then running. Somewhere along the way, I gave up on the running altogether and walked the rest of the way home.

I did this in street clothes—jeans, a long-sleeved sport shirt, a pair of leather dress shoes. God knows what I looked like. People probably thought I'd stolen something, or perhaps killed someone, and was trying to escape. But they left me alone. It was New York, after all, and why interfere?

After a day or two of this, I picked up the phone and called my friend Philip Friedman. I'd met Philip through our mutual agent, and he seemed like an interesting guy, but the one extraordinary thing I knew about him was that he was a runner. He lived on the Upper West Side, and ran every day around the reservoir in Central Park. And he'd actually run a marathon. He was from Yonkers originally, and he'd run the Yonkers Marathon, and that impressed me. (It would have impressed me even more if I'd known anything more about the event than its name. The Yonkers race is one of the country's more difficult marathons, generally blessed with wilting heat and humidity, and boasting a couple of positively oedipal hills. I've never participated myself, and with any luck at all I never will.)

I told him I'd started running, and I wasn't sure if I knew how to do it. He said there wasn't all that much to it, aside from remembering to alternate feet. Did I have running shoes? I said I didn't, and he recommended I go to a store that specialized in athletic footwear and let them sell me something.

I found the right sort of store and came home with a pair of shoes by Pony. I remember that they were blue and yellow, and the most comfortable things I ever put on my feet. I went out and circled Washington Square a couple of times, and when I came home I took off my new shoes and noticed that they had a couple of broken threads in the stitching. So I went back to the shoe store, and they pointed out that the shoes were now used, they showed the effects of a few laps around the park, and they couldn't take them back. And I threw a fit, and to get rid of me they let me exchange them for a pair of Adidas.

That's a good brand, but the shoes I took home were singularly unsuitable. They were running flats, and offered about as much cushioning and support as a pair of paper slippers. They were also a little too small overall, and a whole lot too small in the toe box. It was months before it dawned on me that they were the wrong style of shoe and the wrong size, and that they consequently were so damned uncomfortable to wear. I just thought it was a matter of having to get used to them, and I wore the silly shoes for months, ran all over the place in them, and never failed to luxuriate in the feeling of sheer relief that came over me every time I took them off.

But I didn't let them stop me. I got out every day for my five laps around Washington Square Park. When I went out of town for a couple of weeks in the summer, I found places to run—in parks, on highways, wherever I could get in a half hour to an hour of alternating feet. I never allowed myself to miss a day, because I had the feeling that once I did, I'd give it up forever. I must have missed days when it poured, or when there was ice underfoot. And I remember a snowy day around Christmas when I was sane enough to stay indoors, but nuts enough to lace up my Adidas and run in place in my living room.

I was a runner. It astonished me that I could do this. It's not as though I'd ever spent any time thinking of running as something I might do if I ever got around to it. I can't say I thought much about running at all—for myself or for other people. I knew there were people who ran—I would see them out there doing it—but I also knew there were people who belonged to something called the Polar Bear Club, whose members went out to Coney Island in the middle of the winter and charged like lemmings into the freezing surf. There was no end of people who did no end of stupid things, and what did any of that have to do with me?

I remember standing on Bleecker Street one afternoon, a few doors from my apartment, when someone went tearing past me, running for his life, while someone else—a shopkeeper?—stood on the sidewalk shouting for him to stop. I realized that it was within my power to chase this fellow, that I could quite possibly run him down. After all, I was a conditioned runner. He'd gone by at a good clip, but how long could he keep it up? I could lope along for a half hour, and by then he'd pull up gasping.

Of course I didn't run after the son of a bitch. I mean, suppose I caught him. Then what? But the realization that chasing him was something of which I was physically capable was remarkably empowering in and of itself. A couple of months ago, I couldn't have done it, and now I could, and that struck me as pretty amazing.

I suppose there were physical benefits. This was 1977, which was just about the time when the media were overflowing with the purported benefits of getting out there and jogging. If you put in half an hour three times a week, you were presumably guaranteed immunity from no end of unfortunate conditions, heart attacks foremost among them. Doctors with impressive credentials were going so far as to state that anyone who ran marathons (or, as someone phrased it, anyone who "lived a marathoner's lifestyle") never had to worry about coronary artery disease. He might not quite manage to live forever, but when he did die, it wouldn't be a heart attack that killed him.

This sort of hyperbolic ranting lost some steam when Jim Fixx, a fine runner and a very prominent writer about running, did in fact suffer a myocardial infarction and die in early middle age. It was clear he had a genetic predisposition to coronary artery disease; he'd lost close male relatives to it. He'd lasted longer than the others, and one could argue (and several did) that running had in fact extended his lifespan. Still, it was Fixx's misfortune not merely to die young but to live on as an object lesson for antirunners. For years, any mention of the benefits of running was apt to be met by a raised eyebrow and an allusion to poor Jim. A couple of years ago, a good quarter-century after the fellow sprinted off this mortal coil, I was one of several guest speakers at Mohonk

Mountain House, in upstate New York. I put in an hour or so on the treadmill one morning, then joined the other speakers at breakfast. One of them, a forensic pathologist of some renown, had evidently noticed me on my way to the gym and began taking me to task for it.

"Tell me something," he said. "Do you plan on living forever?"

"No," I said, "though I'm hoping to make it to dinner. I understand there's venison on the menu."

"You people run because you think it's good for you," he went on. "Let me ask you something. Do you remember Jim Fixx?"

"Anyone who ran a marathon ... or lived a marathoner's lifestyle ... ."

When I was circumvolving Washington Square Park, or trotting along some country lane or suburban boulevard, I wasn't trying to live forever. I appreciated the fact that running would take off weight, or at least enable me to eat more without gaining. I'd lost weight during one summer in Florida, but those pounds had come and gone and come again many times over the years. This alone seemed reason enough to put on my shorts and shoes and get out there.

Still, the phrase echoed, and began to do its subtle damage. Not the promise so much as the premise. The one word, really.

Marathon.

To run a marathon. To be a marathoner.

Lawrence Block has been writing award-winning mystery and suspense fiction for half a century. He's also well known for his books for writers, including the classic Telling Lies for Fun and Profit, *and* The Liar's Bible. *In addition to prose works, he has written episodic television (*Tilt!*) and the Wong Kar-wai film,* My Blueberry Nights. *An obstinate if untalented racewalker, he has*

31

completed 20+ marathons, and several ultras, although those days seem to be behind him. He is a modest and humble fellow, although you would never guess as much from this biographical note. For more, visit lawrenceblock.wordpress.com. "It's a Miracle" is an excerpt from his book, Step by Step.

Monkeys and Bonobos

by Jesse Parent

It's my knees, I tell them.
I have bad knees.
An absence of cartilage that hooks
underneath my patella.
Drags remnants down into shin splints.
Straightening my legs
is a new kind of pop and lock.
Years of wrestling and rugby
strip mining my joints.
This is why I can't run.

What I don't tell them is how I still try.
How I beat the pavement in Sketchers
and worry that there is a shoe
I don't know about
that will cast me into a god.
How I hope it's not those creepy toe things.
How I use the Nike app like a video game
because I am obsessed
with metrics and high scores.
How a mile run feels like
I am breathing a damp comforter
into my lungs,
every step a question
as to why I even bother.
Where is this high?
Where are my calves?
Why do my knees still hurt?

Every runner is a bonobo in my monkey world.

I am left to ponder their greatness
and wonder what I lack,
why this doesn't get any easier?
Where are glasnost and perestroika
to tear down this wall?
It doesn't help to convert the miles to kilometers,
an American ignorance of the metric system
I just know it's a long way to feeling
like this isn't work,
like I am getting better.

But I don't stop trying.
I just can't bring myself to tell them
that I am scared.
That my 13 year old son
runs a faster mile than I do,
that I may never reach my goal
of running a marathon at forty,
that my knees may actually give up
before I do.
I am scared I will stop trying
and let the excuse wrap me up
like an afghan blanket,
that feels comfortable, in spite of the holes,
and just watch others evolve into thumbed gods
with toes on their shoes.

Jesse Parent is a poet, an improviser, a former mixed martial arts fighter, a computer nerd, a husband, a father, and, above all, a human being. If you trust the results of the 2010 and 2011 Individual World Poetry Slam, he is also the 2nd ranked slam poet in the world. Jesse is training for his first marathon, and he hopes running will finally let him obtain calf muscles. "Monkeys and Bonobos" is an original piece for The 27th Mile.

Essential Lydiard

by Lorraine Moller

There's a story told about Arthur Lydiard and his golden boys at the '64 Olympics in Tokyo. Down at the training track, with their rivals looking on, they ran an impressive interval session of 20 quarters. The next day one of these opponents, a talented interval-trained Canadian in his first Olympics, showed up at the track with his coach and proceeded to run the same session. Lydiard's boys cheered him on as he ran each interval faster than the last. When it was all done, a reporter asked Lydiard what he thought of the kid's workout. "I think it was the last nail in his coffin," Lydiard replied.

"But your boys ran the same session yesterday."

"Yes, but my boys needed it."

Perfectly peaked, Lydiard's protege, Peter Snell, won two gold medals. His teammate, John Davies, won a bronze. The Canadian who had eclipsed the Kiwis' training run with his own failed to advance to the finals in his event—as Lydiard had predicted.

One of my former coaches, Ron Daws, often quoted the above story to illustrate his axiom: "Good training and bad training look exactly the same on paper." Twenty quarters can bring one runner to his or her peak and bury another in a hole. Daws, adhering to Lydiard's philosophy, recognized that stand-alone workouts mean little; it is their contextual application to the advancement of the athlete's goal that matters. Training, then, is not a series of numbers that can be universally applied, but is rather the art of combining measure, timing, and sequence to the specific needs of the individual. Herein lies the brilliance of the coaching of Arthur Lydiard.

My first coach, John Davies, the same Lydiard protege

who won bronze in Tokyo, called Arthur to ask him how to adapt the training for a promising 14-year-old girl. He didn't want to wreck me. Arthur advised him to build a base by increasing my mileage. I began on regular runs, soon reaching my target of 40 miles per week, which I continued for some months. There were never any of the hard and fast rules that are regularly attributed to Lydiard, such as the 100-miles-per-week mandate, but rather a careful consideration for my age, gender, ability, fitness, and event. And that's how it was for the next 28 years of my career as an international athlete under the guidance of three consecutive Lydiard coaches: Davies, Ron Daws, and Dick Quax. My schedules were never replicated in content; however, the principles that defined them as good Lydiard training (and are outlined in this article) were unwavering.

1. MILES IN THE BANK: MAXIMIZE AEROBIC CAPACITY FIRST

The first phase of Lydiard training is endurance/aerobic development. Think of aerobic running as home base — the place where we hang out until we are mature enough to leave, and the place we always come back to for rest and recuperation. As the miles stack up, we increase the capacity of both the heart and the lungs for work, build our circulatory network to the muscles through increased capillarization, increase the number of mitochondria in the muscle cells, and develop other beneficial metabolic and enzymatic pathways for gathering oxygen and converting it to energy. Once these structures are established, they allow us to respond and recover quickly. Aerobic training, then, is training for all other types of training.

Lydiard often described miles as money in the bank — the more you have, the greater your currency to buy ATPs (the units of energy your muscles need for contraction) and the faster you will eventually be able to race in any event that has a large aerobic component. From the 800 meters on up, the body's energy needs are met primarily from aerobic metabolism, with any race over 5,000 meters more than 85% dependent on aerobic ability.

There is no argument: The greatest gain for any aspiring distance athlete is made by spending the majority of time on aerobic development. And for those recreational athletes training for a weekend road race, this is the only phase of Lydiard training that is initially indispensable.

While easy running is always the safest place to start, it is often the case that the cardiovascular system develops quickly while the musculoskeletal system tends to lag somewhat. The golden rule is that you can never progress faster than your slowest part will allow. Case in point: For the past 20 years, Japanese teams have regularly altitude-trained in Colorado. I often recognized some of these petite women, backpacks on, hiking up the steep incline of Gold Hill some 15 miles out of Boulder. Taking the base-building strategy one step further, the coach had prescribed extended hiking and jogging sessions during year one of the four-year Olympic cycle solely to condition the musculoskeletal system for base building. With strong tendons and ligaments, these runners could then handle up to 200-mile training weeks without injury, and thus develop a superior aerobic capacity.

2. FEELING-BASED TRAINING: TUNE IN TO YOUR INNER COACH

One of the benefits of the buildup phase is that these longer aerobic runs allow you to safely build a rapport with your body. This is a greatly underrated aspect of training, probably because feelings have generally not been a part of any serious exercise discussion. But the ability to precisely gauge one's effort over time is the hallmark of all great athletes. They can run the razor's edge, knowing how to pitch their effort and energy to extract the best from their bodies on any given day.

Lydiard fostered this ability in all his runners by prescribing feeling-based training goals. A typical running schedule would ask for half effort on one day and three-quarters or seven-eighths effort on another. Half effort was half the effort of a full effort, and so on. In the days before heart rate monitors and chronographs, runners simply had to guesstimate until they got the gist of it, which they did quickly.

Modern technology can be helpful training wheels to developing this rapport, but an over-reliance on outside feedback—whether a beeping monitor or a coach bellowing splits from the sidelines—is also a dangerous trap. Ultimately, we are on our own in competition, reliant on the clarity of communication between our mind and our body. I call this the "inner coach," the voice within that knows exactly what we need to do at any point in time to reach our potential. Whether it tells us to back off, relax, pick it up, or make a break, in hindsight it was always the right thing to do. The more we learn to trust the inner coach over time, the stronger its voice becomes.

3. RESPONSE-REGULATED RECOVERY: BALANCING WORKOUTS

Training can be defined as specific stress applied to the body to invoke a corresponding adaptation. The training stimulus (workout) causes a temporary breakdown in the body (catabolic phase) followed by the adaptive period (recovery), during which the body rebuilds itself so as to better withstand the stress that it has just endured (anabolic phase). Break down and build up better than before, break down and build up better than before; this is the rhythm of good training. Interestingly, the desired training effect does not take place during the workout, but during the recovery. We improve not while we are training, but while we are resting.

More often than not, bad training is a mismatch of breakdown and buildup: either the workout is too hard or the recovery is inadequate, or both. (Rarely among motivated athletes is it the result of undertraining.)

The tendency for many runners to overtrain and/or under-recover is underscored by an inflexible training schedule. While Lydiard pushed his runners, he offset the overtraining syndrome by preparing them for optimal recovery with base training, gearing the training to be feeling-based, and adjusting workouts according to the athlete's recovery response. The art of good training calls for an accurate assessment of which side of the adaptation curve the runner is on — catabolic or anabolic — and prescribing appropriately: a recovery run or a workout.

There are simple ways of assessing this: An elevated morning heart rate, poor sleep, low energy, sore muscles, and bad mood are all indicators that the runner needs further recovery, and a workout of any intensity is contraindicated. Once the "spark" has returned, the runner is ready for the next "stress."

Shigeharu Watanabe, coach of Yoko Shibui, whose marathon personal best of 2:19 ranked her No. 7 all-time among women, served his coaching apprenticeship with Lydiard in New Zealand. Of his team he says, "We do only that which is necessary to do, we do not follow any numbers."

4. SEQUENTIAL DEVELOPMENT OF ENERGY SYSTEMS

A study performed by Dr. Izumi Tabata (and colleagues) at the National Institute of Fitness and Sports in Tokyo, Japan, showed that over a six-week period, interval training is more efficient than steady exercise of lesser intensity. Get-fit-quick advocates have quoted this study as proof of the superiority of interval training. What they do not tell you is that anaerobic development takes four to six weeks to top out, and that when it is preceded by endurance and strength training, the possibility of injury is decreased and the quality of the intervals is enhanced.

Whenever Lydiard was asked which part of the training was the most valuable, he always answered simply, "Everything." Often he would follow up with the question, "Who would want to eat a cake half-baked?" This holistic approach distinguishes Lydiard training from one-brand-fits-all formulas, and squelches the quest for the "magic workout." There is no single element that makes one a champion. Rather, what makes the difference is the progressive development of each energy system from low intensity to high intensity, each stage preparing the runner for what is to come next. Speed is built on interval training, which is built on strength, which is built on endurance. When the runner finally reaches her target race, she possesses the entire gamut of adaptive responses, from jogging to sprinting.

5. CORRECT TIMING

Peaking is a matter of correct timing. It is one thing to maximize the amount of energy at the disposal of an athlete. It is another to channel that energy into the event that matters. To ensure that one's best form is achieved on competition day, a Lydiard schedule is always written from the goal backwards, allotting the amount of time needed for each phase and using the remaining time for base training. Thus the training pyramid serves the twofold purpose of physiological and mental focus to arrive at one point in time — the goal. There is no need for a separate mental training program of affirmation and visualization — it is built into the training program. As the athlete gets closer and closer to the top of the pyramid, the training increasingly simulates the race. There is nothing more confidence-building than the somatic knowing of thorough preparation.

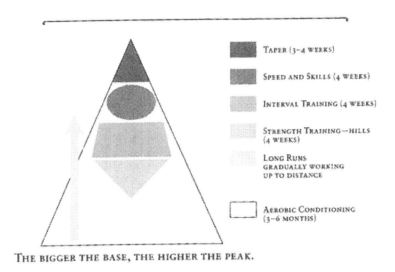

TAPER (3–4 WEEKS)

SPEED AND SKILLS (4 WEEKS)

INTERVAL TRAINING (4 WEEKS)

STRENGTH TRAINING—HILLS (4 WEEKS)

LONG RUNS GRADUALLY WORKING UP TO DISTANCE

AEROBIC CONDITIONING (3–6 MONTHS)

THE BIGGER THE BASE, THE HIGHER THE PEAK.

FIGURE 2:
THE LYDIARD TRAINING PYRAMID

Using the five principles of miles in the bank, feeling-based training, response-regulated recovery, sequential development of the various energy systems, and correct timing, each what, when, how, and why of every action from sleeping to running is another brick in the pyramid that takes one to the top.

Lydiard's greatest protege, Peter Snell, retired with three Olympic gold medals and numerous world records to his name. In his post-athlete career he came to live in the U.S., where he became a doctor of exercise physiology and associate professor of internal medicine. With the eminent credentials of both athlete and academic, who is better equipped to offer a final thought on the relevance of Lydiard today?

SNELL SAYS:

The core of Lydiard training is the quantity and quality of

the base training. Although Arthur appeared to be very precise about the track training leading up to the racing season, I believe this was not as important as the base. Long, moderate-pace running is anabolic, whereas high-intensity demanding training, while having its place, is catabolic. Thus, the base is critical to prevention of overtraining.

Marathon training for an 800-meter runner is difficult for many coaches and particularly scientists to understand. Many have been quite dismissive about the benefits in the face of the outstanding results associated with marathon training. To them it makes no sense training slowly for a speed event. The rule of specificity is violated. Why then does it work? Today our knowledge of physiology provides some answers:

- Long endurance runs appear to provide protection against overtraining from too much high-intensity speed work. Therefore, more race-related training may be accomplished.
- Activation of fast-twitch muscle fibers is normally accomplished by high-intensity interval runs. We now know that long moderate-pace runs also activate fast-twitch muscle fibers, after slow-twitch fibers have become glycogen depleted after the first one to two hours.

In sum, and in light of current physiology, there is little I would do differently today other than incorporate some long, easy intervals once a week during the base training. The training of current top athletes is testimony to the relevance of Lydiard training today.

Lorraine Moller is a native of New Zealand whose highlights as a competitive marathoner include an Olympic Bronze Medal at Barcelona in 1992 and a win at Boston in 1984. She also is a three-

42

time champion of both the Avon Women's World Marathon Championship and Osaka International Ladies Marathon and the only woman to compete in the first four Olympic marathons. After retiring from competitive sport in 1996, Lorraine continued her travels as vice president of Hearts of Gold, raising money through running events in Japan, Cambodia, and Mongolia. Presently she is president of the Lydiard Foundation, helping bring the Lydiard training philosophy to future generations. Her autobiography, On the Wings of Mercury, *was published in 2009. "Essential Lydiard" was originally published by* Running Times.

All You Need Is a Thumb

by Chris Cooper

I'm through with lonely, boring mile repeats on the local high school track. I'm saying goodbye to 20-mile long runs on Saturday mornings while others catch up on their ZZZs. I now have no need for tempo runs, maintenance runs, hill runs, fartlek, striders, tapering, dynamic stretching, cross-training, training manuals, hydration, carbo-loading, energy bars, gel, Gatorade, logging mileage, mileage schedules, mile pace charts, breathable clothing, orthotics, running watches, running singlets, or pricey running shoes, thank you very much. Oh, and that treadmill in the basement? The missus always wanted a drying rack … Merry Christmas honey!

Which, of course, means no more blisters, popped hamstrings, blackened toenails, twisted ankles, swollen ankles, tendinitis in the ankles (okay, no more ankle *anything*!), chapped lips, chafed nipples, nausea, runner's diarrhea, sore quads, sore knees, sore calfs (or is that calves?), vomiting behind bushes, vomiting on my shoes, fearing the wall, hitting the wall, or just trying to get to the damn wall in the first place.

See, I've been doing it wrong all these years and so have you. And so has a friend of mine who is approaching her 100th career marathon. What have you and I and her (or is that *she*) been doing wrong all these years? We have been *running* our marathons! Gasp!

Thankfully, I have finally seen the light thanks to the inspiration rather than perspiration of Rob Sloan. Not too long ago, Rob completed a prestigious marathon in England not by training for it and surely not by suffering in it. No. He did it by taking the bus. Sloan took an easy stroll for about twenty miles, hopped on a spectator shuttle bus, and emerged from the woods right before the finish line to make the podium. Gotta love those Brits!

Okay, okay, I know what you're thinking … you're not a bus person. Fine. Neither am I.

So, what do you do? Be like Rosie and take the damn subway is what you do. In 1979, Rosie Ruiz, that heroine of couch potatoes everywhere, took the A-train to Columbus Circle before walking to the finish line of the New York City Marathon in Central Park. But here is the genius part: she knew enough about subway timetables to *achieve a qualifying time for Boston* while doing it.

I mean, think about it. You too can BQ without all the prep work. And isn't that especially critical now that the qualifying times are five minutes faster than before? Damn right it is. We'll show that holier-than-thou Boston Athletic Association we won't be manipulated!

Who's with me?

That's right. No more running in the rain to get in your weekly mileage. No more packing your running gear for that business trip so you can do a lap in the hotel parking lot. No more being chased by Rover ("Oh, he won't bite") over hill and dale. And no more inhaling car fumes from running along the shoulder of the road (although in Pittsburgh they call it the berm … and we say soda and they say pop. Go figure).

Of course, after Rosie tried a similar strategy to "win" the Boston Marathon the following year, witnesses came forward saying they saw her dash onto the course in the last mile. Hey, I didn't say this is foolproof.

Not convinced? Not a problem. There's one more option and all you need is a thumb. You heard that right, a thumb. I got 'em, you got 'em, we all got 'em, and monkeys don't got 'em … or so they tell me. And what you do with that thumb is hold it out by the side of the road and wait for a sympathetic non-runner to pick you up and take you to the finish of the nearest 26.2 mile race.

Preposterous you say? No freakin' way you say? Then you better read up on your Olympic heroes is what *I* say. No, not that Shorter fellow from Yale. A *real* hero. A *real* inspiration. A Fred, not a Frank. At the 1904 Olympics, probably because he didn't have bus fare or a subway token, American Fred Lorz used good old American ingenuity to hitch a ride eleven miles to the end of the race in time to pick up the bronze medal. USA! USA!

Don't believe me? Look it up, I'll wait.

Okay, he was caught too, but forgive and forget is what I always say, and that's just what happened. Good old Fred was forgiven and allowed to enter the next year's Boston Marathon. But (yes, you knew there was a "but" coming) not every story has a happy ending, especially this one. Sure, Fred WON that Boston Marathon ... but he had to do it *on foot*.

Chris Cooper is a sub 3-hour marathoner, a Boston Marathon finisher, and author of the book, Long May You Run: all. things. running. *He lives and runs in West Chester, PA. For more, visit chriscooperonline.com. "All You Need is a Thumb" is an original piece for* The 27th Mile.

Running with Buddy

by Chris Russell

Nobody loves to run more than my puppy. His name is Buddy. He's less than three months old.

When we run together, Buddy hangs back on the uphills—his little legs can't eat up the ground as fast as my long stride—but on the downhills he blows by me like a furry, black and white cruise missile. His pace is incredibly smooth and efficient. He hugs the ground, ears back for speed and no wasted effort.

In December I brought home a sad little bundle of fur from a business trip to Tennessee. He was so small and quiet that I had him in a small soft-sided pet carrying bag under the seat on the plane and no one even knew. This fur ball was to become my favorite running buddy. He is a professional friend, and he is very good at his job.

Buddy loves to trot a short three-quarter-mile trail loop with me. He beats me back every time. He's not even breathing hard. He's definitely designed for it. I think he likes it. I stop and let him do doggy things if he wants. I'm very relaxed in my dog-parenting style.

I don't drag him on a leash. He's unclipped and free to quit at any point, but he doesn't. He knows the trail loop. He knows where he is in relation to home.

He dogs me on the way out, staying close on my heels. Then, when we turn the corner to head back on a narrow and winding downhill section, he turns on the jets. He knows he's heading back. He cuts the corners on the trail and leads me in.

He doesn't sprint and zigzag like a Labrador, crashing around the woods in exuberant lunges. He's a Border Collie and I'm a giant lost sheep that he's leading home. He keeps a steady pace and conserves his energy. He keeps to the trail and is never more than two or three paces ahead or behind me.

He has a beautiful stride. He doesn't look like he's running. He flows over the ground with very little vertical pitch.

He is extremely agile. He has learned how to get over the fallen tree trunks that block the trail. He times his leaps just right and uses his momentum to easily vault obstacles that are as tall as he is. He takes them in stride like an Olympic hurdler, never disrupting his pace.

He's an inspiration to me, my running Buddy, because running is a natural act for him. In contrast, only a few humans make running look natural. Many (myself included) look decidedly unnatural, like we're fighting gravity, making our bodies do something that they weren't designed for.

I think too much about the mechanics, the purpose and the meaning of running. Not Buddy. He looks good. He sets an enviable example with a pure, guileless, unthinking and unencumbered approach to the action of running.

It's a striking contrast. It has taken many years of physical and mental machination for me to experience the 'joy' of running. But this little fuzz ball was born with it. He doesn't run to lose weight. He doesn't run to get in shape. He doesn't run to relieve stress. He doesn't race. He runs because it's his nature. It's what he does.

He dreams about running. How many of us can say that? (Aside from that recurring nightmare where you show up for the marathon but have forgotten your shoes?)

This running dog has even affected my non-running wife. When she takes him for walks on the same loop, he pulls at the leash and wants to jog, especially when she turns the corner and heads back. He can't understand why she just won't jog a little. In his world view, he wonders why the heck anyone would want to walk?

I can't imagine what he going to be like when he grows up. How are my paltry 10k jogs going to satisfy him? He's just a puppy and he's already got more gears than I do. I guess he'll just have to wait for me to catch up. I can picture him as a two year old sitting in the trail ahead looking back with pity on my plodding.

Like all new babies, he has begun to show glimpses of the adult to come. He is very much changed from the tiny fur ball that I carried back on the plane with me in a little bag. You couldn't fit half of this dog in that bag!

I didn't get the puppy to have a running partner. I got a puppy for my kids. It is coincidental and fortunate for both him and me that we have this thing in common: a love of running. We'll take it one day at a time and see how it goes. I'm not going to push him into any distance until he grows up. Maybe he can be trained to push me out of bed for my long runs on Sunday morning when it's cold and forbidding outside. (A warm tongue to the face in the pre-dawn hours?)

The next time you go out for a run, remember Buddy and run like a dog. Approach your run like it is something you were born to do. Flow over the ground with an easy, unthinking and natural stride. Enjoy it for what it is and not what your oversized brain reads into it. And when you return, dream sweet dreams of herding fat, happy sheep in a bucolic land where to live is to run.

Chris Russell lives and trains in suburban Massachusetts. He is the author of The Mid-Packer's Lament *and* The Mid-Packer's Guide to the Galaxy, *short stories on the human comedy of the mid-pack. Chris' podcast,* RunRunLive, *is available on iTunes and at www.runrunlive.com. Chris is a member of the Squannacook River Runners and the Goon Squad. "Running with Buddy" originally appeared in* The Mid-Packer's Lament.

The Long Haul

by Ben Tanzer

Chicago, IL, January 2010

The smart thing of course would be to not run today at all. Last night I went to listen to Ike Reilly at Schubas, and I drank many beers. I got home late and, after watching television and gabbing with my wife for an hour, I didn't sit down to write until 2:30 in the morning. That got me to bed at 3:30 in the morning, and then I was back up at 7:30 to get the boys ready for school. After that it was time for my annual physical, for which I have been fasting since midnight, clear liquids only; I am allowed to drink coffee, but have not.

At the physical I give blood, and have a prostate exam. Sweet. I walk to the supermarket, so I can help my wife carry the groceries back to the house. We get home and watch the latest winner of *American Idol* perform on Oprah. I am hungry, tired, and sluggish. It is now almost noon, and I still haven't had any coffee. I held off on eating so I could run, which I expected to do much sooner. The smart thing of course would be to not run today at all.

And yet, I can eat later. I can sleep later. I can drink coffee later. But there's no guarantee that I will be able to run later. Shit happens. I'm gone.

There is a long run that has been my standby for the fifteen years we have lived in this neighborhood, but between work and family, I haven't hit this one as regularly as I normally would. I'm going to hit it today, though. I head up Dearborn and into Lincoln Park, past the famous Saint-Gaudens statue of Lincoln himself, and down through the underpass where the homeless reside during the winter and the spiders spin their big-ass webs all summer.

I am excited about this route after having had a break from it, but it's a tricky run for me in many ways; or, well, maybe just one way. After all, it's not a hard run, and there are no hills or weird terrain. There's almost no traffic and, as a whole, the running paths are wide and free of bikers and dogs.

No, the problem is psychological. During our early years here, this run took me about 52 minutes on a good day and in more recent years it's taken closer to an hour; last winter, due to a combination of an arthritic knee and sleep problems with the boys, I ended up going through one of the worst stretches of running I've ever experienced. Eventually things got better – the boys' sleep problems seemed to fade, and I also learned that my arthritis was being exacerbated by the Merrill Wigwams I used to obsessively wear – so one night when I went on the run, I decided to time myself.

67 minutes.

Fuck. I knew I had been running slower, but I wasn't ready to actually be *slow*; or worse, accept that I'm getting older and that some of this is inevitable. I also didn't think I had to go down without a fight. Did I?

I am now passing the Latin School soccer field and wrapping onto the footpath. I run along the lagoon where the scullers row morning and night, and where the geese stop over during their annual migration to wherever it is that they go. This run has four evenly divided sections to it; after recording my sad old-man 67-minute run, I decided to start trying to get as close to fifteen minutes for each section as I could. It still wouldn't get me to 52 minutes, but it would at least be closer to an hour, and that, I've decided, I can live with.

67 minutes quickly became 62, and then grudgingly became 59, then 58, and on a good day 57. And then one morning during the fall, I hit 55 minutes. It was completely triumphant and completely crushing all at once; because

although I was happy with the time, I just didn't feel good. Not when I finished, not after I showered, nor all day at work. My back was sore. I felt queasy. And there was some chafing that just doesn't happen at slower speeds. Worse, though, was the thought that I simply might never be able to replicate 52 minutes again, but that I would obsessively try, because any time I did this route I would wonder whether I just wasn't trying hard enough, adding a psychological blow to whatever weakened state would result from my attempts to achieve whatever had transpired that run.

I head under the second overpass of the run and pass the unofficial fifteen-minute mark, though I have decided against looking at my split times for each of the sections because I don't want to get depressed. I am pain-free, which is always nice, but I am not spry, although I don't know if this means anything for how the run will end. I never feel wholly good during the first quarter of any run, at any distance; I am still not loose, and my head is still not completely in it. Another thing affecting me today is not just this invisible bar I've set for this particular route that now haunts my every step, but that I never even try any more to run fast on any other route, and so I haven't attempted to run fast at all for months. Further, it's light out, and all sunny and warm, none of which is conducive for speed, not for me anyway.

I pass the driving range and head in closer to the lake, approaching the totem pole at Addison and the halfway point of the route. There are a lot of runners out today. I can see them out of the corner of my eye, and I can feel one of them coming up on me. I would like to tell you that I don't mind being passed, that this is not a competition for me, but I would be lying. When this guy finally passes me, I pick it up a notch. It does not feel good. Not bad necessarily, just not good. There's no electricity, no juju, and while I may not be bonking, I just don't have much in the tank today either. I start to obsess over the fact that I must be tired, that I'm not hydrated or caffeinated, that I have given blood and that I'm not even quite halfway done. Motherfucker.

Luckily, I am juggling multiple obsessions today; I have also been talking to a literary agent for the first time. It is terrifying, though not because of any particular fear of being rejected, which is always a bummer but is also an incessant part of being an artist, and thus best to simply ignore. No, I am more freaked out by the fact that she may want to work with me. Or, strike that; she *has* been working with me, but I'm freaked out by the fact that it might be successful. What then? I don't think I overly pride myself on being an outsider, loved by just a few readers here and there, having nurtured my writing outside the world of MFAs, workshops and conferences; this is simply how it's worked out for me, and is the path I've chosen to take.

Okay, maybe that's somewhat disingenuous, and maybe I do enjoy whatever "outsider" status it is I think I possess, but I don't think it's been holding me back or making me less ambitious, has it? I always thought the whole effort was about improving my craft and seeking opportunities, and that, like with running, when my skill level and the right opportunity converged I would grab it. Which is what this agent represents, an opportunity that I am thrilled by, have grabbed onto and don't plan to let go of.

I make the turn for the second half of the run and start working my way back home. I know I've picked up the pace, but I can't tell how much. I still feel terrible, and in the daylight I can never quite get my bearings anyway. I try not to obsess over blood and food.

I sent the agent a mostly final draft of what I like to believe could be my third novel. It's the story of a guy who is married and trying not to sleep with his intern. He's also scared to have a baby and would prefer not to kill his neighbor. More than that, however, he's smart enough to know that he should be more curious about his life and his decisions, that he shouldn't be so reflexive in his decision-making, but he can't quite get there, instead losing himself in his confusion and his failure to communicate what this means to him and those around him, until things get shaken up with the birth of his child and the child's subsequent medical struggles.

I pass the three-quarter mark of the run and I have a decision to make. This part of the route, which directly follows the lakefront from Fullerton to the North Beach footbridge, is where fast runs go to die. I either hit this part with everything I have left, going for broke and trying to come in under an hour, or I let myself start to fade before I even reach the final stretch onto Dearborn and home. I decide to go for it, pumping my arms and pushing forward.

My legs immediately feel sluggish and my breathing turns erratic. Spittle starts to fly from my mouth, and my nose begins to run over my lips and onto my collar. My chest starts to throb, and some weird cramp begins to crawl from my right shoulder into my neck. I am actually seeing stars and begin to wonder whether I am going to pass out. Why didn't I eat? Why did I go out at all? Why am I pushing myself like this? My form starts to break down, my arms jerky and my legs stiff. This is a bad place for me; this is where my knee is most at risk of becoming inflamed. By the time I reach the footbridge, I am having trouble breathing.

The agent thinks my dialogue is authentic and my characters are real. She seems excited about the book. But she wants to talk plotting. Is the story too predictable? Are there subplots lacking closure? Maybe. Maybe I can do more with the hot opera-singing neighbor and her rockstar ass. Maybe I can show more interaction between the various couples in the book as the story evolves. And maybe the pregnancy itself can be explored in more depth. Maybe there are a million things I can do if I think she's right and trustworthy and I am willing to take the plunge, seize whatever opportunity ultimately emerges, and push myself farther than maybe I am comfortable with. Maybe.

I pull up in front of our apartment building and look at my time. 56 minutes.

Fuck yeah.

Ben Tanzer runs. And when he doesn't run, he writes. The novel mentioned in this piece was published as You Can Make Him Like You. *For more, visit bentanzer.blogspot.com, the center of his growing lifestyle empire. "The Long Haul" originally appeared in Ben's collection of running essays,* 99 Problems.

All the Way to San Francisco

by Willy Palomo

I used to love reading. For years, I believed I was actually going somewhere, had no idea I was only living vicariously. I thought I could breathe every petal, blooming like face, on wet black bough. I thought I was Alice, Wonderland and all. But now every page I turn feels like the wing of bat and I'm all Goya. You'd be surprised to realize just how empty your life is once you decide to stop living vicariously. So much of what we do is imaginary: books, television, video games, text messages, Internet, mathematics, history — turns out half of the intellectual pursuits aren't real. Suddenly all the big, stupid buffs who used to slap each other's asses during football and strut around the halls of high school grabbing their junk all day all seem like geniuses. Even music feels like audio pornography. You can't get away from it. You don't know what to do with yourself. Suddenly even love feels too abstract, floating over my head in a colorful storm of Pollock, Stella, and Kandinsky.

I'm not sure how to tell you this, Somel. I can barely open my eyes right now, but I'm writing you this letter. I have never loved someone so much that even the pen I am writing with feels unreal, a love angry as gasoline boiling in my throat. I see you in my mind the same color as sand, where the sky crashes over you, clouds and sun and birds and all. My love is drunk as Kerouac, listening to *Howl*, a holy, holy, holy bursting from your tongue like a naked Jesus. Anyone can talk about Rumi, Camus, and revolution, but by the end of the night, you had me wishing I could leave with you to San Francisco. I never watched the dawn rise like I did next morning, breathing the Albuquerque air searing in the heart of the desert, filled with an agitated calm, a wild peace that rivets in my blood like war. I work overtime licking envelopes, try selling my poetry through drive-thru windows, trying to make enough money to go to San Francisco.

Once I met you, I made a vow to start living again, to stop living vicariously and feel everything again all at once all the time. All for myself. There are nights I can't sleep just enjoying my existence, feeling the cold grass lick at my back as I sweat myself wet beneath the heat of the moon, where all the stars of the night surround me like flies around a carcass. I feel dead-alive, like I'm asleep, watching the evening close over me like the velvet lid of a coffin, gorgeous and black as Sartre's Negress. I don't want to do anything anymore. I don't want to read another book only to learn that no amount of fire or freshness can amount to what a man hides in his ghostly heart. I don't want to watch another movie only to realize that I can't press rewind again, again, again, and again. I won't listen to another song. I don't want to keep imagining you anymore.

I think I'll go running this evening.

In the darkness.

All the way to San Francisco.

Willy Palomo is a student, a performance poet, and a man who loves running. His work has appeared in ellipsis…literature & art *and* Scribendi. *He will be representing Salt Lake City at the 2013 National Poetry Slam in Boston. "All the Way to San Francisco" is an original piece for* The 27th Mile.

Vanishing Act

by Julie Greicius

In Las Vegas, we spent a blistering four hundred dollars — a hundred bucks each for my husband, our two kids, and me — to see a famous magician. A fifteen-minute montage of endorsements by other famous people told us this magician was the greatest magician we'd ever see, the greatest magician of all time, the magician who changed magic.

The crowd exploded in applause when he stepped onstage. His cool blue oxford shirt billowed unbuttoned over a white T-shirt and black pants. His hair was full and black. He was funny, charming and eminently confident. His posture cried out, *You're welcome.*

He started out easy, asking a volunteer from the crowd for her wedding ring. He hid it in his back pocket; seconds later, he returned it to her, knotted into the laces of a baby's shoe. Next, he stepped into a giant fan and emerged in a puff of smoke at the center of the theater. Each trick was bigger than the one before. He made a 1948 convertible appear out of thin air. He cast Frisbees into the audience, asking each person who caught one to answer a question. *How many children do you have? How many hours has it been since the last time you had sex? What size are your boxers?* Their answers added up to a series of numbers. He told a long story about his now-deceased grandfather not wanting him to be a magician. At the end of the story, he lowered a clear, fiberglass case from the ceiling where it had been hanging since we first arrived, opened the safe that was inside it, and took out two license plates — from his grandfather's '48 convertible, he told us. The numbers on the plates were the exact numbers, in order, that the Frisbee-catching audience members gave him in their answers. What, he asked, would his grandfather say about

61

him now?

I wanted in on this thing. I sized the place up—how I'd catch the next Frisbee, or catch his eye, or somehow stand out so that I, among all these adoring hundred-dollar ticket holders, would be chosen. Like everyone else in the room, I wanted to get as close to the magic as possible.

I saw my kids and husband staring up at the stage, their eyes glistening with reflected stage light. I imagined what life would be like as a magician's assistant. I was sure I had the intelligence to be a real creative partner, a co-conspirator—a small career reassignment that would have done my restless soul some good. I wanted to be part of the magic, but more—I wanted to *be* the magic, turned into something, cut in half and put back together, placed in a box and run through with swords—to triumph over the physical world. I wanted the magnificence, to have my full potential tapped and treasured, and then to stand, one hand in the air, smiling as I took a bow.

What he would do, instead, was make me disappear.

He was not the gentleman magician whose acts revolved around a stunning, subordinate beauty—brains or no. His illusions required an army of highly skilled assistants each of whom worked with the zeal of an apprentice and the devotion of a groupie. I wondered, for a moment, what kind of person would set up his world this way—a sun around which everything revolved but from which everything must remain at a distance.

With their help, he lobbed a dozen silver exercise balls into the audience. They drifted through the dark auditorium. The willing reached up and plucked them out of the air. The unwilling sprung them gently back up off their fingertips. I, desperate to be part of the trick, climbed hungrily over the row in front of me to grab one.

He called out to the ball-catchers to hurry toward the aisle and onto the stage. I climbed over legs in seats and got in line behind the others, holding my giant ball. An assistant grilled every volunteer before allowing them onstage. She spoke fast. *Are you a reporter? Are you a magician? Do you have children in the audience?* I looked at my family, and back at the woman. "No." And then the last question, which seemed to come not from her but from the gods: *Can you run?*

Could I run? The better question might have been: could I do anything else? I'd run hundreds of miles against breast cancer, against brain damage, and for my own health nearly every day of my adult life. Two decades on trails and sand and pavement. In snow and pouring rain. While pregnant. While injured. I ran everywhere I lived, from the suburban streets outside Philadelphia, to the streets of Manhattan, around the Central Park reservoir, to Boston, along the Charles River Esplanade, and in the foothills of Northern California. I ran in every country I ever visited, from France to Fiji, believing that I couldn't really know a place until I'd run its streets and trails. And now, perhaps, Vegas.

If running was the trick, then I was the magic.

She let me pass and I climbed the stairs onto the stage. The floor was black, marked with bright tape and a list of words in white letters that glowed along the front edge — an inventory of every trick he had performed that evening.

The magician asked my name, then spoke to me — *Julie* — as the other volunteers took their seats in a dozen chairs. He told us to wave goodbye, then pulled a silver curtain around us. Through an opening in the curtain, the magician handed me flashlights. "Julie," he said. "Take these flashlights and pass them to the other volunteers. Everybody gets a flashlight." He handed me the biggest flashlight of all — like a searchlight — and told me to wave it back and forth. A chaos of moving lights played across the curtain.

He continued talking, and the laws of physics bent to his words. I was twinned, two possibilities existing at once.

I dashed through a blur of black curtains and bustling assistants. They gave us no directions, just pointed down the street. *Go!* It was a fine command, and one I could fulfill. I was off like a bullet, suddenly running along a dark street in Las Vegas. I had no idea what street I was on or where I was relative to the other streets around the casino theater. I dashed out ahead, hoping to do right by this trick, because when that lady had asked me if I could run, I had thought she meant *run*. I looked behind me and saw a few other volunteers shuffling in the distance. I worried about the quality of this illusion with an earnest sense of duty.

I'd never been much for running in the dark, except as a child of 11 or 12 when my older sister took me out to keep her company. We jogged through our suburban neighborhood on humid summer nights. Every 100 yards or so she'd shout, *"Grand jeté! Grand jeté!"* — switching us from simple steps to great bursting leaps, infusing the whole thing with a kind of playful ecstasy that forever defined running for me. And it became my foundation: *If I can do this, I can do anything.* I learned to be patient, take the steps, and let them add up. I learned to scale hills, lean forward, and push off my toes and past my limits, whispering: *I've got so much more than this; I've got so much more than this.* I told myself I'd get to the top of the hill by foot or by ambulance — and it was always by foot. I grew to trust the bliss after the brutal apex, because after body temperature, blood pressure, pulse and respiratory rate, pain is the fifth vital sign. I learned never to ask myself whether or not I wanted to go. Only: *Go!*

I ran down a long street that seemed unusually dark for Las Vegas, and found myself suddenly alone in an unfamiliar place. I looked ahead and behind me and saw no one. There was someplace I was supposed to go — and fast — but I didn't know where. My regular routes had always been trusted loops, where I could forget about place and focus on movement—meditation in motion. Every circle, as Rumi wrote, was a zero. Perfect emptiness. When I ran I wanted to vanish—from work, from parenthood, from adulthood, from responsibility, from the confines of the indoors into the endlessness of outside. And now, in the middle of this magic trick, I had done just that: vanished.

Where were the rest of the volunteers? Should I go right or left? A moment of panic washed over me. With nothing else to go on, I went forward. I reached a corner and looked down a long alley. A man dressed like a magician's assistant stood under a light by a door.

I ran in his direction. He smiled as I approached, standing by as if waiting to hand me a cup of water at a mile marker. He directed me inside and pointed down a hallway. I rushed forward, through backstage corridors and a huge kitchen, down another corridor, and into a tiny room with a television monitor. Surely, it was the strangest run I'd ever been on. I was glad to sit down.

Soon, five other volunteers showed up. I wondered what might have happened to the others, but there was no time to worry. Another assistant walked in and started a lightning-fast lecture. *Here's what the audience is seeing,* he told me as he gestured to the monitor. *Here's how the trick works.*

Here's what you can tell people when they ask you how the trick works. He presented diagrams. *My god,* I thought. *They've thought of everything.*

To anyone who's ever suggested that a person can't be in two places at once, I would say: you've never met this magician. I was still onstage in a giant silver-curtained box, lit from the inside with all our moving lights. My husband and children watched the stage. My flashlight and moving silhouette signaled to them through the curtain: *I'm still here.*

Backstage, between the spontaneous race I'd just run, the four complicated diagrams, and the anticipation of where I was trying to imagine I'd end up after I leaving that room, I couldn't possibly form any realistic memory of how the trick worked. I was trying to pay attention, to figure it out, when the magician himself walked in.

I wondered how he, too, could be in both places at once. He smiled and shook each volunteer's hand. As a gesture of appreciation, he gave each of us a gorgeous, glossy 8x10 headshot, boldly marked with his signature.

A scale took shape in my mind, and I weighed the delight of sharing this adventure against the delight of keeping his secret. What I found at the center of the scale was gratitude. It was the summer of my small orbit, the closest I'd get to this sun.

Sure, this magician had walked into a fan and made a car appear out of thin air, but what could he do with a dozen untrained volunteers sitting and waving flashlights? He pulled the silver curtain down. A giant puff of smoke exploded over a dozen empty chairs. He aimed a searchlight at the back of the room and shouted, "Audience! Look behind you!" They turned and found us standing behind them in the back rows, shining our lights around the room and onto their dazzled faces.

The audience gave a standing ovation. The magician bowed profusely. Then the lights came up. In case anyone was still uncertain, the montage of flattering quotations replayed on the screen as the crowd filtered out of the auditorium.

In the lobby, my family wanted to know everything. My husband laughed, and my children clawed at me anew. *How did you do that?* I smiled and told them, "My legs are magic."

Julie Greicius has been a runner for 22 years. She is editorial director at Lucile Packard Children's Hospital at Stanford, senior literary editor at TheRumpus.net, and co-editor of the 2010 anthology Rumpus Women. *"Vanishing Act" is an original piece for* The 27th Mile.

Running Home

by Amby Burfoot

I'm on vacation at my brother's cottage near Long Island Sound; it's less than a mile from the home where I grew up. I have run the nearby roads so often — for 50-plus years — that I recognize every crack in the asphalt. This one, a sort of "Y" on its side, means that I am approaching the 1-mile mark. It's just 20 or 30 yards ahead.

The crack with the grass in the middle is just past the 3-mile mark. If I subtract 10 seconds from my time there, that's close enough.

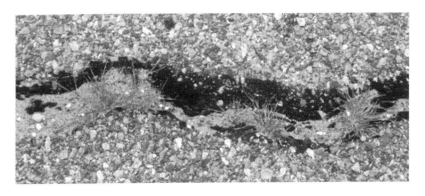

The grass changes to a double crack with seashells at the 5.5-mile mark. These cracks are located just a few yards from the most sparkling beach you can imagine. When I hit this point, I've got just a half-mile to go.

Then, finished with my 6-miler, I can jump into the chilly waters, just as I have done for 50 summers and more. I can't stay in long; I'm too skinny for that. But I flutter-kick for a few minutes on the assumption that this will loosen my tight leg muscles, and prevent injury. I have no proof for this method. But, like I said, I have been running here for 50-plus years.

Something seems to be sustaining me.

These roads, and the familiar cracks, give my life a sense of permanence. I know it's a lie. After all, I won't be running here in another 50 years. But for now they provide more comfort than I can possibly tell you. I almost feel that things haven't changed.

The tides reinforce this feeling. My running loop traces the perimeter of a true peninsula; it's surrounded on three sides by the Sound's lapping waves. As I make my way around, there is water immediately to my right or left about 75 percent of the time.

When I was young, we followed the tides closely. We judged them by scanning the rocks near shore. When they were exposed enough for us to see barnacles and greenish-brown seaweed, it was low tide. When the rocks nearly disappeared, and we could see only the upper 10 percent, like the tips of icebergs, we knew that high tide had arrived.

At low tide, we waded into the shallows, wiggled our toes into the soft bottom, and dredged up clams for dinner. At high tide, we dove from the docks, and swam to and fro without icky eel grass scratching our legs.

Fifty years later, improbable though it seems, the rocks are right where they've always been. I see this clearly as I run my favorite loop, now three minutes per mile slower than in days of yore. Low tide and high tide look exactly the same as when I was 12. The water comes in, and the water recedes. All is right with the world.

Like many, I worry about climate change, melting icecaps, rising oceans, and the environment we will leave to my children's children. But when I run on the edge of Long Island Sound, where I have always run, I have little cause to ponder global warming.

Instead, I am struck by the immutable cracks in the road and the eternal ebb-and-flow of the tide. I know things always evolve. But for now, I am happy—almost delirious—to be enjoying yet again the same simple and little-changed run I have enjoyed for a half-century.

Amby Burfoot, a Runner's World *editor-at-large, won the 1968 Boston Marathon and has finished the Manchester (Conn.) Thanksgiving Day 5-miler 50 years in a row. For more, visit www.ambyburfoot.com. This piece originally appeared on runnersworld.com.*

Something to Run For

by Ray Sespaniak

Steve was sitting on the couch watching the news on TV after getting home from work. His leftover turkey had cooled off, but Steve barely noticed. He was too busy talking back to the TV.

Today it was the vote in Congress on the tax bill that set Steve off. "You can't do that!" he exclaimed, shaking his fork at the screen. A forgotten slice of white meat bounced off the anchor's face. "Do you think we're all stupid?"

After the commercial break, a blonde "lifestyle anchor" appeared on the screen to report that more than a third of American adults were overweight. "That's awful," Steve muttered, gnawing on a drumstick. He burped and looked down at his waistline, which reminded him that he was part of this particular problem. Taxes, war, unemployment—Steve couldn't solve those issues, but he could do something about his weight.

The lithe young thing on the TV had a solution for his situation: exercise. She listed a number of workout alternatives. Running looked like an inexpensive, easy, and convenient way to get some exercise, compared with paying for a gym membership or finding a group for sports like tennis or basketball. Steve decided to give it a try.

On Saturday, Steve went to the local Wal-Mart and bought a cheap pair of training shoes. He went home, grabbed a T-shirt and an old pair of shorts, and went out for a run.

Steve barely made it to the end the block before he had to stop. "This sucks," he thought, hunched over with his hands on his knees, breathing heavily. "Running's a lot harder than it looks." When he got his breath back, Steve trudged on for a little longer, but by the time fifteen minutes had passed, he was done for the day.

Steve was sore the next day, so he plopped down on the couch to watch the Sunday morning political interview shows. It wasn't very restful. Shows were either pointlessly argumentative ("Why is it that the only job sector in our national economy that is fully employed is Village Idiot?") or just plain stupid ("We can cut taxes and increase services!"). He channel-surfed for more than an hour before giving up in frustration. "Might as well go for another run," he muttered to himself. "It can't be any worse than this!"

Steve's progress was sporadic. He'd run one day, then skip a day or two before he went out again. But he never quite stopped. There was always something in the paper, online, or on TV to make him angry, and he'd put on his shorts and shoes and go for a run to work out his frustrations.

After a few months Steve realized, that without consciously deciding to, he had started running almost every day. He looked forward to his run, and if he had to miss a day, the next day's run came as a relief. His extra weight was gone and for the first time in years he felt good about his appearance. He had more energy and he had more endurance when his friends asked him to play softball, go bike riding, or go for a hike.

Most importantly, running helped Steve relax from the stress created by the barrage of human foolishness that continually bombarded him. Wherever Steve went, whether to the local coffee shop for a drink, to the garage for an oil change, or to the mall for a pair of pants, there was always a radio playing or a TV running, spewing out streams of bad news and foolish opinions. Running was always work, but there were moments while he ran where Steve managed to forget the nagging annoyances of the world.

Steve started looking for more ways to work running into his life. He signed up for his first race, a 5K in his hometown and surprised himself by finishing 3rd in his age group and taking home a trophy. After the race Steve was trying to enter his results into his exercise log on his smartphone, but something was keeping the app from responding. Then an ad for diet potato chips popped up, with a smiling model stuffing his face covering the screen. The only thing that kept Steve from smashing his phone against the wall was that he needed it to start planning his next run.

When Steve was in the middle of a race, running as hard as he could, the effort and concentration drove any other thoughts out of his head. Soon 5Ks weren't enough. Steve began running longer distances. Inevitably, that led to Steve signing up for his first marathon, Marine Corps in Washington DC. Training for a marathon took up a lot of time, but the goal kept him focused on his running, and helped him ignore the waves of information clamoring for his attention.

After a few more big city races, Steve tried a marathon in a smaller city, and he found that he liked those races even more. The events were more about the running and less about selling the marathon experience to runners. There weren't as many people cheering him on, but the races weren't as expensive and the courses weren't overcrowded. Soon he was signing up for obscure marathons, and running races on quiet roads and trails with maybe a few hundred others there to keep him company.

Steve was at one of those small marathons, in South Hero, Vermont, when he met an older runner who told him about even longer races called ultramarathons. More miles? That sounded good to Steve. That conversation led to Steve spending Mother's Day in Ipswich, Massachusetts, running a three-mile loop in the woods as many times as he could in eight hours. Steve took it easy, but he still managed to complete 39 miles.

By this point Steve's whole life revolved around his

running. He would go to work, come home, run, eat, and go to sleep. On weekends he would get up early and use the extra time to go on longer runs lasting for eight to ten hours. He'd read an article pointing out that not one Wall Street financier was charged with a crime after the mortgage scandals and economic meltdown, and he'd just shrug and tack an extra five miles onto his daily run.

Steve tried to explain his running to his soon-to-be ex-girlfriend. "Running calms me. When I'm running I can escape for a little while from the all the stress and suffering that surrounds me. I can get lost in the drone of footsteps and forget for a little while how much pain there is out there." She told him that she also felt forgotten when he was out running, and when he didn't argue with that, she left.

It wasn't about running fast anymore. Steve found it much more enjoyable to relax and see how far he could run. He often felt a little anxious when he wasn't running, but his daily run took care of that.

Steve signed up for a 50 mile race in Vermont in the fall. He finished, though he had to struggle through muddy trails created by a continual downpour. When he tried his first hundred mile race, Steve only ran 70 miles before he couldn't go any farther and dropped out. That just reinforced his resolve. He tried the same race again a year later, and this time he finished in just under 24 hours and earned a silver belt buckle. After that, whenever Steve found himself in a political discussion, he'd usually rest one hand on the buckle and run his thumb over the top edge with a faraway look in his eyes.

The tipping point came after a shorter race, the HAT Run 50K in Maryland. That close to Washington, it was inevitable that Steve would run into people discussing politics after the race. They were arguing whether health insurance should cover injuries that kept people from running, but didn't affect them otherwise. Given why he had started running, Steve was going to argue the point, but his legs felt fine and it was a beautiful day, so he decided he'd avoid the debate and run back to his hotel instead. After all, it was only 20 miles away.

When he got back to the hotel, Steve showered and had dinner. After eating, he tried to relax on the bed in his room and watch a movie. He surfed through the channels, but all the movies he found were interrupted by ads every few minutes, and it seemed like every other ad featured a disturbing clip from that channel's 11 o'clock news. Each ad made Steve a little more restless, until he turned off the TV and picked up a book. That didn't keep his attention either. He thought about heading down to the hotel bar to see if there was anyone to talk to, but he couldn't face another political discussion.

Finally, at about 10 o'clock Steve decided he might as well do what he usually did when he felt edgy. He changed back into his running clothes, grabbed a bottle of water, and went out for a run. A quick five or ten miles and then he'd go back to the hotel and sleep.

Almost immediately after starting, Steve felt better. Ten miles flew by. Steve returned to the hotel, but instead of going up to his room, he decided to keep going until he felt tired. He ended up running until dawn, finally stopping when he needed to get back into the room to shower, pack, and check out.

The eight-hour drive home crawled by. Steve kept shifting in his seat. He usually passed the time on these trips by listening to music on the radio, but there were so many interruptions for ads and news programs that he gave up and turned it off. When he stopped to eat, he thought about pulling his running shoes out of the trunk and going for a short jog, but that seemed silly. Instead, he got back in the car and resumed driving.

Steve found himself driving faster and faster. He made a

conscious effort to slow down, but whenever he glanced at the speedometer, he'd see that his speed had crept up again. He could hardly wait for the drive to be over.

At last Steve pulled into his driveway. He unpacked his car and started the laundry. He still felt edgy, so he decided that a run would be just the thing to work out the kinks after the long drive.

Steve took off, and ran his standard 26-mile loop. When he returned home, he had a bite to eat. Even though it was evening, and Steve had done more running than usual, he still wasn't winding down. Steve decided that since he felt good, he might as well put in a few more miles. He figured another ten miles would do it, but when he finished ten he still wasn't ready to stop so he went out for another ten miles, and another after that.

After he finished the third ten-mile loop, Steve figured that he could quit for the day. By this point, he'd been awake, either running or driving, for almost two entire days. While this wasn't unprecedented for Steve, it was usually something he only did in the course of an ultramarathon. But enough was enough. Steve showered and went to bed.

He lay down and waited to doze off. Instead, the restless feeling began building up again. Lying in bed felt pointless. Steve didn't really feel the need for rest. He felt like he needed to be moving, that he had to get away. Steve struggled with this for a couple of hours, tossing and turning. Then he gave in. He slipped out of bed, put his running clothes back on, and headed out the door.

Steve ran through the night. He made it back home after dawn on Monday morning, just in time to shower, dress, and head to work. By the time he drove to the office, he was already feeling the need to get out and run again.

The first thing on his calendar was a weekly staff meeting. Steve managed to sit through half of that meeting before he got up, told the others he wasn't feeling well, and left for the day. On the way out, he stopped by his desk and took out the spare running shoes and shorts he always stored there. When he got in his car, he changed into his running gear, hopped back out, and took off.

Steve ran until noon. He stopped for a snack, and then ran for the rest of the day.

Somewhere in the middle of the afternoon, he began to worry a little. Physically, he felt fine in spite of all the running. He was a little tired, but comfortably so, the way he would feel in the middle of a 50 mile race. But he knew he should be more tired. He'd been running for most of three days! This level of endurance was the sort of thing he had dreamed of, but it was a leap in fitness that was outside of his experience, and more than a little weird.

At the end of the day, instead of getting his car from the lot at work, Steve put his concerns aside and ran home. He grabbed a bite to eat and, almost automatically, reached for the remote to turn on the TV to watch the news.

The next thing he knew, he was back out on the street, running. Steve stumbled for a step, then fell back into his smooth running stride while he tried to figure out what had happened. Apparently, he had gone into some sort of fugue state between the time he had turned on the news and the time he came to his senses. Steve checked his pockets. He found he had taken his keys, some cash, his phone, and his credit card before he left the house. His legs felt great.

He didn't understand what was going on, but it seemed like it wasn't doing any harm, so he just kept going. Soon running calmed him down, the way it always did.

At midnight, Steve circled back home. Again he tried to sleep, but just as it had the night before, his mind kept spinning while his body flopped back and forth, looking for a comfortable position. His compulsion to run made him uneasy, but when he tried to get his mind off the running, his thoughts were tangled and confused. He was angry at the events in the media and how people didn't see the obvious solutions to the problems; he was disgusted at the stupidity of the people who elected the crooks and believed the obvious lies; he was frustrated that there wasn't any way to get people in power to listen; he felt guilty that he wasn't doing everything he could to help whatever he could; he felt afraid of the consequences if the problems weren't solved and sad that people were suffering unnecessarily... until the pressure to get up and run away from his thoughts pushed him out of bed and back on the road.

Steve struggled for days. Every time he stopped running, to eat, try to sleep, or just sit and talk with someone, the restlessness began building until the compulsion to run took over. His doctor gave him sleeping pills, but they didn't help. They just made him dangerously fuzzy-headed when he gave up trying to sleep and went back to running, so he stopped taking them.

Finally Steve accepted what had happened. He put together a small knapsack of essentials, quit his job, told some friends his plans, and then struck out with the intention of running until the compulsion went away. It didn't seem like he had much choice in the matter. He just hoped his obsession would run its course before his money ran out. He tried not to think about what would happen if he got hurt and couldn't run.

Steve quickly settled into his new routine. Every morning, Steve stopped to eat breakfast and pick his next destination. Then he'd settle into a groove and spend the day running in a half-focused, meditative state. Some days he'd stop to do laundry or take a shower if it was convenient. But most of the time, he just ran.

He ran at a steady pace that averaged out to about ten

minutes per mile. At times, he'd develop a blister or some minor aches and pains, but he was able to walk those off. Somehow, he managed to avoid any major injuries.

After a few months of continual running and some worried calls from his family, Steve started using his phone to post updates on his travels to the Internet. He began by simply posting his location to a service that automatically built a map of his travels. Then he started to put up pictures and notes to share details of what he was doing.

Running helped Steve get away from the hectoring voice of the media, but he found couldn't avoid it entirely. Often, one-sided political commentary or reports of earthquake devastation drifted to him as he ran, along with the noise from traffic or the smells of barbecue on a summer evening. Even the "free" apps he used on his phone nagged at him. Every time he went online to check his mail or post an update, there were a few more ads tugging at the edge of his awareness.

Other runners heard about Steve's trek and passed the word. A small online community gathered around Steve to follow his ramblings. On his walking breaks, Steve read their comments and posted responses.

His fans helped him out by pointing out places where he could get water, go to the bathroom, charge his phone, or find a supermarket with free food samples he could use for a quick snack.

The support from his followers let Steve strike out on longer trips, slowly making his way across the country. He planned his route to stay in the temperate zone, going farther south in the winter and back north in the summer. That way he only needed to carry shorts, singlets, shoes, socks, jocks, a cap, and sunglasses, along with a little money and his phone.

His steady pace allowed people to plan to meet Steve and run with him for a while. Everybody wanted to know what it was like to be able to run as much as he did. He told them,

"I'm always tired, but when I try to rest, my mind starts spinning and I get edgy. It's like I've always had one too many cups of coffee. The only thing that seems to help is when I run."

Sometimes he'd stop with a temporary companion to eat. A few times, he hit it off with a woman and they went to bed. There, his endurance was also great, sometimes too great. And he wasn't much for cuddling afterward, because by the time they were done, the compulsion to run had built up again and he had to leave. Eventually Steve started turning down similar offers. As much as he might hope for an encounter that would turn into a relationship, he realized that if he couldn't manage an entire one-night stand, anything more was unlikely.

Steve's fan base grew. He made charity appearances, and he even managed to make a little money from race appearance fees. His story went viral for a little while - at one point, six of the top ten videos on YouTube showed people in costumes running alongside Steve. But the attention wound down. Within a year Steve was back to being, at most, a minor curiosity. His following contracted, though he retained a core group of runners and ultrarunners who helped him out when he needed it.

Daily, Steve wondered if his compulsion to run would ever end. He had no need for lodging, and there were still plenty of people willing to stake him to a meal, so his money wasn't running out. But in spite of all the people he met, Steve was lonely.

Springtime came around again. Steve's annual drift north had him running through Massachusetts when he received a message from the Central Vermont Runners asking whether he wanted to drop by Montpelier for their Tuesday night fun run. He checked his GPS and figured that he had plenty of time to cover the distance to Montpelier before the next evening and, with nothing better to do, he emailed back to say he was coming and turned north.

After the run, Steve went into town with a few of the club regulars for some Mexican food at Julio's. The news was showing on the TV at the bar, so Steve sat with his back to the TV, which put him next to an attractive woman. He introduced himself, and she told him her name was Eleanor.

Over tacos Eleanor told Steve a little about her life. She worked as a home health aide, visiting people's homes and helping them with their medical problems. Steve admired the way Eleanor obviously cared about her clients and wanted to do whatever she could for them in spite of the low pay and heavy caseload.

Eleanor was familiar with the basics of Steve's story, but when she asked, he went into more detail. Steve tried to gloss over the loneliness and focus on the interesting characters he'd run with and his gratitude toward the people who'd helped him out.

Then the sound from the TV sliced through the conversation at the table. Steve winced when he heard a reporter was talking about cuts in school health programs.

"Something wrong?" asked Eleanor.

"It's the idiots on the news," Steve said. "I don't know what bothers me more. The fact that they're fighting over cuts to programs that hardly have an impact on the budget, or the fact that they're reporting this instead of something that's actually important, like the war."

"It's just TV. It's all about the ratings. People don't want to have to think after a long day at work. They want to watch news and pretend they're informed, but they really only want to see spectacles and stuff that confirms their view of the world."

"Why can't people do simple math?"

"Everybody's the same way," said Eleanor. "You're no different, Steve. You look at the news and see what you expect to see, and you let it make you mad. Sure, the stuff you see on TV or the Internet is usually angry, scared, or stupid. But look around you. Is that really all there is? You spend a lot of time out in the world, more than most people. The people you were telling me about aren't mean and stupid. Why let the bad stuff drag you down? Stop and smell the roses, or the sweaty shoes, or whatever it is that makes you feel good, not bad."

Eleanor smiled and put her hand on Steve's. "You like running, don't you?"

"Actually, yeah," said Steve, distracted by her touch. "Though I'd like to have some choice about it, at least take a day off here and there."

"Well the world, that horrible world you live in, is the same world that's made it possible for you to run everywhere and manage to survive doing what it is you do. Have you asked yourself why you can't see that the good that lets that happen along with the bad? That there's still a balance? Sure you have to push against what's wrong in the big picture, but you also have to stop and enjoy the small picture, which isn't always bad, right?" Eleanor squeezed Steve's hand, then let go. "You seem to think that you're responsible for doing something about all the problems of the world. What a silly man."

Steve raised an eyebrow in acquiescence and smiled back. None of this was new to him, but when Eleanor said it, it felt different.

When dinner ended, Steve and Eleanor hugged and said goodbye. Steve thought about asking for her phone number, but the pressure he felt to run dissuaded him, and regretfully he headed back out on the road.

Still, in the long, empty stretches between his contacts with others, Eleanor kept popping back into Steve's thoughts. Three weeks later, he gave in and wrote the CVR events coordinator to let them know he'd be back in Montpelier for another run.

When he arrived that Tuesday, Eleanor was in the group waiting at the start of the run. Suddenly Steve felt both hopeful and awkward, like a teenage boy on a skateboard peering from the deck of a halfpipe for the first time. He walked around greeting people he knew, stalling, but by the start of the run he was next to Eleanor.

"Hey."

"Hey you," she replied happily. Steve relaxed, the run began, and soon they were chattering comfortably, undisturbed by passing miles or passing runners.

Steve quieted as they approached the parking lot where the run ended. Eleanor noticed and asked if something was wrong. "Not really," said Steve. "I just wish that sometimes I could stay in one place for longer than a meal or a quick chat."

"Well, you never know. The world might be a bad place, but in spite of everything it brought us here tonight. Right here, right now isn't too bad, is it?"

"I'm not sure I want to count on the world to make this happen." Steve teetered on the coping of the pipe, then leaped. "If I come back in a week or two, would you want to go for a run?"

Eleanor stopped and looked at Steve for a moment. When she grinned, it was like he'd hit a backside 180 for the first time. "Why not? We can take fate into our own hands for a change."

Before long, Steve found that he was staying in the northeast and planning routes that let him get back to Montpelier every week or so to meet Eleanor for a run. Steve loved how nothing ever fazed Eleanor. He found that he could disagree with Eleanor without having it turn into an argument. Whatever the subject, she could always put a positive spin on it.

Eleanor, in turn, was charmed by Steve's naive desire to

fix everything. He badly wanted to help, but he was overwhelmed by all the problems he saw, unable to focus on any one of them, an Albert Schweitzer with ADHD. She was serenely confident that one day Steve would learn to focus and make better use of some of the energy he spent on running, and she hoped to be around when he did.

Late in August, after another evening run that ended at Eleanor's house, Steve hugged Eleanor and was set to say goodbye when Eleanor gave him another one of those looks. She asked if he wanted to come in.

Steve wanted to, very much. But he wasn't sure whether it was the right thing to do. "Are you sure that's what you want?" he asked. "Soon it'll be fall. When it gets colder, I'll be heading back south and I won't see you anymore, for months at least. It's not fair to ask you to wait for me. And even if we do get back together, we can't really be together since I always have to get up and go."

"You still worry too much," said Eleanor. "I'm enjoying your company now, and if you stop coming back when winter comes, well, I've been dumped before. I don't let it keep me from hoping, and enjoying the good moments when they occur.

"Look, it's late, I have to work in the morning, and I'm tired. Why don't you come in? I need a shower, and you could use one too, road-boy. Then I'm going to bed. You can lay down with me and keep me company for a few minutes while I fall asleep. Leave whenever you have to, I'll be fine."

Steve followed Eleanor into the house. They showered, had a snack, and then went into Eleanor's bedroom. She set her alarm, and then they got under the sheets. Eleanor kissed Steve goodnight, then curled up on her side. "Hold me, Steve." He did. "Mmm. That's nice. G'night."

Steve lay there, with Eleanor warm in his arms. Soon her breathing deepened, and he could feel her relax into a deep sleep. It felt right to start breathing along with her, trying to get just a little closer before he had to leave. He shifted until he could feel her heart beating slowly against his forearm. "Just another minute or two, then I'll have to get up and leave," he thought. He took in a deep breath, inhaling her scent, then released it and shifted slightly.

"BRRRRING!! BRRRRING!!"

Steve sat up abruptly. What was that? Why was it light all of a sudden?

Next to him Eleanor stirred and stretched an arm toward the nightstand. The sound stopped. She looked up at Steve and said, "Oh good, you're still here. Give me a kiss and then I'll get up and make some coffee."

Steve realized what had happened. "I slept," he muttered, slightly dazed.

"Yes, you did," said Eleanor. "Did you know you snore? Now kiss me, and let's get going. It's time to start another day."

Ray Sespaniak has run the Vermont 100 almost one-and-a-half times. His articles on running have appeared in The Boston Globe, Ultrarunning Magazine, Marathon & Beyond, The Christian Science Monitor, *and other publications. For more, visit y42k.com. "Something to Run For" is an original story for* The 27th Mile.

The Runner

by Ben Tanzer

"What the fuck," Landry says to no one in particular on the first day of high school track practice. "Is he going to be like this all the time?"

Landry with his feathered hair and pigeon-toed strides is the golden boy miler and undisputed leader. I hate Landry already and I know that will never change; when hate takes hold, you have to learn how to live with it. If not it corrodes and so do you.

I also love him, though, which is the way it is with people who are so much cooler than you are.

There is also Landry's sidekick, Donnie, ramrod straight, eyes forward, one step behind Landry, always; and Ron, my sort of friend from the neighborhood, with his wispy mustache, slight frame, and eager-to-please countenance.

"No, Landry, he's cool," Ron says, pleading. "Seriously, and he's going to buy some real running shoes—right, Lee?"

I'm running in my canvas Nike tennis shoes. I don't know about running heel-to-toe or anything else. I just know that running makes me feel alive and indestructible as I slap the road with every step, the sound echoing across South Mountain where we keep silently and rhythmically climbing as the sun sets, the sweat settles in a light film on our backs, and the sky stretches across our home town of Two Rivers like a shadow.

"Yeah," I say quietly. "I'm getting new shoes."

"Good," Landry says. "Now the shut the fuck up. This is a sacred space, and we are gods."

Landry may or may not be a god, but we treat him as such; we have to.

This is in part because he is a miler and there is nothing

89

more glamorous than that. It is also the hair and the dazzling white teeth, neither of which anyone of us knows how to obtain, and his facility with women — even the mere fact that he will talk to them at all is mesmerizing for us.

Ultimately though, it is his fierce competitiveness that most holds us in his thrall. He is not scared to compete: every race is seen as something to be deconstructed, owned, and controlled. For him, to race is to live, to win is glorious, and we fear doing anything that will get in the way of this, or him.

So maybe we are not gods, but he just might be.

Of course, to be a god is to be flawed, and to think you can control anything is to eventually control nothing at all. And so it is with Landry, no sense that rivals can emerge, no sense that they might even exist.

There we are at a dual meet, though not even an important one, some lame-ass high school and us, when Donnie somehow beats Landry in a race.

Landry doesn't say anything. He just walks away. Just like that. This doesn't seem like Landry, and it isn't.

"It's not loaded," Landry says the next night as we sit in his car after practice and he pulls out a gun. "Here, check it out."

I don't want to check it out.

"Take it," he says, semi-smiling, semi-not.

I take it.

"I want you to wave it around Donnie," Landry says. "In private, and then tell him that you think him winning that race was not cool, not fucking cool at all."

"It was one race," I say, taking the gun, and feeling its heft as I pass it from hand to hand and then lift it into the air and point it towards the setting sun.

"That doesn't matter," Landry says.

"I don't want to," I say. "This is stupid."

"You're a pussy, bro," he says reaching for the gun.

I hate him for being weak and flawed, and for being human, and hating Landry for these things is so much worse than hating him for being superhuman.

If he is just like the rest of us, what are we?

We are nothing.

He grabs the barrel, and I pull back, not ready to give it up, and not ready to give into him. It goes off. Just like that. And Landry's dead, slumped over the steering wheel, not moving, no nothing really, except for a little trickle of blood working its way down the side of his face.

There is a moment when I feel a sense of relief and freedom, but it's quickly replaced by fear and regret and the sense that I should just run off into the woods, no pause and no explanation. No one would question that.

But I don't, I can't, and so I pause, and soon people are running towards the car, and my path is set for me.

No one asks what happened — later they will, but outside of the police, no one ever asks directly. The gun belongs to Landry's dad and it was an accident, it had to be.

That is enough to explain it.

Well, that and the belief that sometimes you cannot explain these things. There are no reasons, and no true solace.

There is no punishment either except for the punishment I subject myself to.

Because that moment, the gun firing, the sound of it echoing in that enclosed space, the shattering of eardrums and lives, that does not fade, not ever.

I cannot sleep. I cannot look people in the eyes. It's all too much. The memories following me across the years, the guilt, and the constant smell of gunpowder that never quite goes away.

Even the smallest noises resonate in my head as gunfire.

So I run, always, measuring steps, counting miles, punishing myself with this solitary pursuit, as I try to outpace the shadows ever creeping across my bruised mind.

Out there, on the road and trails, where there is no anger, no sadness, just one step after another.

And so it goes, day after day, month after month, then years, until tonight.

There is a storm, the storm of the century they're calling it. People are encouraged to stay inside and avoid the constant rat-tat-tat of the rain, the downed power lines, and fallen trees.

But I can't stay in, and I won't, and my heart is pounding at the mere thought of it.

I lace up my shoes and head into the hills, through the woods, the lightning crashing like bowling pins all around me.

The air is electric and I am aglow, like a god, a fallen god rising from the ashes.

I head onto the road that bisects South Mountain, arms pumping, jaw loose, and eyes nearly closed by the incessant rain hitting me in the face.

There is a moment, where the lightning and the crashing and everything around me threatens to take me back to Landry's car, but I am distracted by a couple of bears ambling across the road, and I am struck by the fact that they are glowing, bathed in the ethereal light that emanates through the storm clouds overhead.

I slow down to take in the majestic sight before me and see that there is a car overturned in a ditch by the side of the road that is slowly filling with water. There are two men inside, one lying peacefully across the steering wheel, the other banging on the window.

My inclination is to keep running. No contact, no emotion, no pain. But I pause, and after that my path is clear, and it is one of my choosing.

I climb down the embankment and wade into the chest-high, murky water, the rain continuing to pound my head.

I lean towards the window, cup my mouth with my

hands and shout, "I have to wait until the car is totally submerged."

The sound of my voice is startling to me, covered with dust from lack of use, and sounding like someone else's completely. Someone I don't know, someone not me.

When the car is fully submerged, I remove my top layer, wrap it around my fist and punch the window until it breaks.

As the water surges into the car, I unhook the man's seatbelt and he floats out to me, like a baby, bloated now, and unconscious.

I drag him to the road and begin CPR, then mouth to mouth.

How long has it been since I touched someone else?

He starts to cough, then breathe, rolling over and spewing out the buckets of water previously sitting in his throat and lungs.

When his eyes go wide, and his life has returned to him, I shake the glass out of my top, put it back on, and run off into the night.

Later, I am sitting on my back deck, the sun not yet up.

I run compulsively, endlessly, suppressing my hate, my fear, any and all feelings about Landry, competition, what's right and wrong, and how fucked up things can get.

I wear the right shoes. I measure my heart rate. I track every mile, the time of year and day, and the conditions I run in.

I run because I have to, because something was switched on and that's the end of it.

I run early in the morning or late at night because that's when I choose to do so.

I make sure I have no contact with anyone, ever; that's the way it has to be now.

The coffee is brewed, I'm drinking it black, sip after sip, the heat searing the back of my throat, and I'm lacing up my shoes.

I look up and a deer is there, right in front of me, slowly breathing in and out, its massive frame undulating before me. We lock eyes; his are inky, impenetrable, and, as he begins to turn away, I rush to finish tying my shoes.

I take one more swig of coffee, run my fingers through my recently graying hair, and when the deer heads back into the woods behind my house, I go with him, keeping pace, never too close, but matching breaths as the orange yolk of the sun starts to ooze across South Mountain, melts into the valley, across the Susquehanna River, and passes through town before quietly moving on to somewhere else.

I finally lose the deer in the thick of the woods way off above the house, but I keep climbing into the sky, one step after another, same as it always is, and always will be.

I don't believe in gods, fate, luck. Shit happens. The universe is fucked. We persevere because we run, and sometimes we even get to feel joy.

Like this morning.

Ben Tanzer runs obsessively, in spite of an arthritic knee. He is the author of several books, including the upcoming novel Orphans. *For more, visit bentanzer.blogspot.com. "The Runner" is an original piece for* The 27th Mile.

Baby Birds

by Willy Palomo

I find too many baby birds this time of year.
Every morning, I stop jogging to nestle one
back in a bush, its parents chirping like sirens
overhead. From a distance their music would

still sound more like Mozart than anything else.
Sometimes my ears can't tell the difference
between a symphony and a dirge. I always find
them too late. The first few days they resemble

dog paws, still as a child, asleep on the sidewalk.
I pass, a skip in my step, as if I were dodging
a stone, careful not to wake them. The following days,
I watch as feathers spread like the tufts of a dandelion

into the wind. Eventually, all that's left is a brown
skeleton, a plucked hand of grapes. I keep running,
remembering nature's way, God's plan, how my body
is just as much dirt as a bird's. I keep running.

Can you hear its siblings whistle overhead?
Can you tell me whether they cry or sing?

Willy Palomo is studying English at Westminster College. He has represented Westminster College in the 2013 Collegiate Union Poetry Slam Invitationals. Willy uses his poetry to motivate him to run faster.

We Who Watch

by Joe Henderson

When asked to add my byline to *Marathon & Beyond*, I quickly agreed. But then I privately asked myself: Do I really belong there? Readers were justified in asking the same: How well can he speak to our interests?

They were right to wonder about my credentials, not as a writer but as a runner. They ran marathons, and some ran beyond that distance. My life as a marathoner had sputtered to a halt in 2000, after four dozen finishes (including four Bostons) spread across four decades. I wasn't yet ready to say that my last one had been run, but the passing years had turned a probably-soon into a maybe-someday. Meanwhile my life as an ultrarunner had never taken me far, as I'd dropped out more often than finished those few races, all run by 1971.

Which returned us to that question: Did I have anything left to say to runners of distances now available to me only in aging logbooks? Yes, I decided, justifying my new position in *M&B* by broadening the definition of "beyond." It didn't have to mean only "longer than." The word could also imply "in addition to."

"Beyond" could include runs other than marathons and ultras, the shorter training and racing that isn't devalued by the long. "Beyond" could include what happens after the long racing is finished, when the knowledge of and appreciation for marathoning and ultrarunning don't end at the final finish line.

Paul Reese, the grandest old man of the roads I know, once bristled when I referred to him as an "ex-Marine." Colonel Reese corrected me by saying firmly, "There's no such thing as an ex-Marine." He explained that once you've had the experience—and Paul had it in three wars, from the 1940s to the 1960s—it never leaves you.

Likewise, there are no ex-marathoners or ex-ultrarunners. Once you join this club, you never really leave. The experience stays with you, to share with the runners who follow you on these courses.

Those of us who stand and wait also participate. If you go to a marathon to support the runners you know, to wait for their faces to appear in the crowd, then you are involved too. Watching can stir your emotions in same ways that running does, and sometimes more.

In your own races you have at least the illusion of control. But you can't run your friends' miles, which is why you worry for them. Running for yourself, you focus on the little steps right in front of you, and on those just taken. With friends, you see how far they've come to get to the marathon start, and you know how getting through 26.2 will change them in ways they don't yet know.

Each year I watch former students of mine, from running classes at the University of Oregon, graduate into marathons. They took their early steps with me, then passed their final and most vital exam by continuing to run on their own. At their marathon start I feel more nervous for them than I felt before all of my own marathons combined. At their finish I shed more tears for them than for all of my races.

We who stand and watch also serve. We cheer the runners who do what we once did, giving them the support that we once received. We show the passers-by that what they do does not go unnoticed or unappreciated. No one knows them better than one who has passed this way before.

Exercises in Patience
My day in Portland, Oregon, started with an early wakeup call—not from an operator downstairs at the Hilton,

but from the next room. This had to be a marathoner. Who else would be so busy and noisy before dawn on a Sunday morning? My wakeup at that hour wasn't unwelcome. I too wanted the 7:00 a.m. Portland Marathon start to hurry up and arrive.

I wouldn't run a step this day. Sunday is my usual day off from running, a traditional if not Biblical day of rest each week. All I had to do at this marathon was watch others complete a journey begun months earlier.

Runners throughout this hotel woke to the day they'd planned for and worried about all year. I looked out the window an hour before starting time and saw runners warming up on the dark streets. As they wasted steps that would be needed later, their impatience was showing.

This restlessness was contagious, as I also left the hotel too early. While walking to the start area, I passed a church. Chiseled in concrete on one wall was the line, "Run with patience the race that is set before us." I wasn't religious enough to know if this was a line from the Bible. (It comes, I learned later, from Hebrews 12:1.) But it spoke clearly and wisely to all runners, and especially to marathoners. Marathons are exercises in patience. Gratification is long delayed.

The hardest part of the race is getting to the starting line, which is why so many more people say they'll run a marathon than actually do it. The months of training test a runner's patience. Injuries and illnesses happen, weather turns uncooperative, family and job conflicts arise, training partners drop out. The patient runner keeps training.

More testing of patience comes in the final several hours. Notice that if you split the word "patience" in the middle and drop a few letters you get "pace." These two running virtues are this closely related. Race day becomes an exercise in pacing, when a runner intent on averaging 9-minute miles must fight the temptation to start at 7s and risk an early exit.

At the Portland Marathon start, I watched thousands of marathoners pass by. I had stood talking with a stranger but now broke off the conversation as a choke came to my voice. Back at the hotel a little later, my wife Barbara asked, "Did you see anyone you knew at the starting line?" I mentioned just one by name.

After thinking about this response, I amended it to include the thought that had choked me up earlier: "You might say that I knew all the runners by what it took them to get here, what it will take to get through their marathon, and what they will take away from this day as lessons and memories."

Three Cheers

The viewer gives encouragement to the runners, and also takes inspiration from them. Having favorites to support adds to the thrill of watching. No one in the National Capital Marathon in Ottawa my one year there inspired me more than Ernie DeCaro from Auburn, New York. The year before, he had undergone cancer surgery that had taken the gluteus muscles of his left buttock.

His condition was serious, but he could still joke, "I now have official certification that I'm a half-assed runner." He had run and raced for years, but had never tried a marathon until New York City eight months after his surgery. After finishing, he wrote, "My thoughts go immediately to next time."

National Capital came next for Ernie. After corresponding for more than a year, we met for the first time at this race. We walked from the expo to our hotel on Saturday, splashing through a rainstorm. I told Ernie, his running partner Cathy Troisi, and our mutual friend Larry Sillen, "We're almost there."

Cathy said, "That sounds like one of the lies that

spectators tell you during races." Sometimes they shout specifics, such as, "Only one mile to go." Distance and time are elastic. Early miles seem to pass in a few minutes each, while the last mile feels a half-hour long. A related lie is, "It's all downhill from here." The last mile always seems uphill, no matter what the topo map might say.

My favorite lie: "You're looking good." No one looks his or her best at the end of a marathon, especially a rainy one. You're not supposed to look good. This is not a beauty contest or a style show, but a survival test. Olympic marathoner Don Kardong once wrote, "Want to see how you'll look 20 years from now? Glance in a mirror right after you finish a marathon." A rare truth-telling spectator asked me late in one race, "Are you okay? You don't look so good." I must have appeared to need a 911 call.

Cathy Troisi recalled a sign that a woman held in the late miles of a New York City Marathon. It read, "Remember, you chose to do this." And runners even paid for the privilege of pushing themselves this far.

At Ottawa I took a position about a kilometer from the finish. The view was closer to the runners there than at the finish line, and the voices were quieter. Most of my cheers stayed neutral: "Way to go." "Good job." Or I just clapped. It doesn't matter what's said there, if anything. Runners only want to know that someone, loud or silent, cares what they're doing.

When Ernie DeCaro passed, I had to shout: "Almost done … downhill from here … looking good!" Considering how far he'd come back, this was all true.

End of the Road
The scene after the finish line of a big marathon, the first moments after the last running steps, is startling to the uninitiated. Finishers have made their final push for the line

and their last gestures to the crowd. Now they start to walk away from it all, as well as they're able.

An observer can't help but notice the people who look the worst. They wear a thousand-meter stare, unaware of anyone nearby. They limp, stagger, weave, or lean on other runners for support. They bend double from pain or fatigue. They bleed or vomit.

Officials triage the cases, sending those most at risk to the medical tent. The others shuffle toward the comforts of space-blankets, drinks, and foods. An ugly scene, you say? Only if you don't look beyond the suffering. If you do, you'll come to see the finish line—past it, not in front—as a strangely beautiful place to watch a race.

I sometimes stand there. That was my view twice in as many weeks one autumn. Casual visitors usually are as welcome in the chutes as they would be in a busy emergency room. The serious business of results-taking is done here, and even the runners are hustled away as quickly as possible. But special passes let me get in everyone's way at both the Portland and Victoria Marathons.

Les Smith, the Portland director, conducts a seminar each year for other directors. It ends with an invitation to observe any and all facets of his operation. I don't direct any race but took great interest in this one. About a dozen of my students were running, along with many more friends. What better place to greet them than at the end of the road?

Rob Reid taught me this. He directs the Victoria Marathon in British Colunmbia, where his habit is one I'd like to see copied by other race directors. He stands just past the finish line to shake runners' hands and thank them for coming. Rob invited me to join him at the finish.

You quickly get over any squeamishness or sense of intruding on a personal moment. The runners don't seem to care how they look or act, so why should you?

Here you see them at their most honest, all poses stripped away. Their hair and clothes are a mess. The young look older, and the old, ancient. Here you see the whole range of emotions and actions. Runners shout, swear, shrug, smile, or sob. You can't tell right then if these are expressions of relief, defeat, or joy.

I'm invisible to most of the passers-by, and rightly so. But sometimes one will respond to the good wishes. Lorne Sundby is an acquaintance from Edmonton. I'd met him only a couple of times before, at other finish lines. In Victoria, Lorne gave me a sweaty hug and yelled, "I qualified for Boston!" I was honored to be with him at that beautiful moment when efforts began turning into memories.

Joe Henderson contributed for more than 40 years to several magazines, while also authoring many books on running. In 2004, he began coaching a marathon training team, which gave him dozens more reasons to stand and watch races, and inspired him to train for and complete more marathons himself. For more, visit joehenderson.com. "We Who Watch" was adapted from a column for Marathon & Beyond.

The 27th Mile

Rejoice! We Conquer!

by Cristina Negrón

One afternoon in late June, my stepson, Dan, showed up at the door of my home office. He was living with my husband, Amby, and me for a few months since returning from a three-year stint in Japan, where he had graduated with a Ph.D. in robotics. Dan spent most of his time holed up in our guest room working on a book on advanced mathematics. After he finished, he planned to move to Cambridge.

"I want to tell you something," he began. "But you've got to promise not to tell anyone else."

"What?"

"You promise to keep it a secret?

"Yes, yes. What is it?"

He raised first his left eyebrow, then his right, in his signature Dan fashion. "I'm thinking about running the Athens Marathon with Dad. Maybe you could do it, too."

"What? What?????"

A year earlier, Amby had signed up for the October 31 Athens Marathon (along with his brother, Gary, and brother-in-law Bill) but had been thinking of the event far longer than that. The Athens Marathon commemorates the most famous day in marathon history, when in 490 B.C. the fabled Greek messenger Pheidippides ran roughly 26 miles to Athens. He started from the town of Marathon after a brave band of Athenian soldiers won a battle against a much larger invading Persian army, who threatened democracy and lots of other good stuff we now hold dear.

According to legend, Pheidippides announced the victory but didn't live to provide any details. Apparently he blurted out "Rejoice! We conquer!" and died on the spot. Like Pheidippides, runners in the current Athens Marathon also start in Marathon and finish in Athens—but in a magnificent marble stadium, built for the first modern Olympic Games in 1896. And most of them don't die after crossing the finish line. The 2010 race would be the 2,500th anniversary of the "first marathon."

For Amby, a former Boston marathon champion (1968), the anniversary event tugged at his heartstrings. For me, a former marathon finisher, not so much. Ever since giving up marathons in 1999, I'd been far more focused on making sure nothing tugged at my hamstrings. When Amby sent in his entry form, he needled me just a little: "Are you sure you don't want to run Athens?" I'm positive, I had answered. I was never going to run another marathon. I said I wanted to go to Greece, of course. I would happily cheer for him and Gary and Bill at the finish line, along with Amby's sister, Natalie. Natalie and I would be cheerleaders in Athens. It had long been settled. That is, until Dan unsettled it.

Dan's idea had only two problems: me and Dan. I hadn't run a marathon in 11 years. I'd become a fitness runner, never going longer than five miles. Although Dan ran occasionally, two or even three miles now and again, he'd never done a road race of any distance, much less the big one. Neither had Amby's daughter, Laura. It would be the sweetest, most memorable occasion of Amby's life, I thought, if one of his kids ran a marathon with him. The fact that the idea had come from the imagination of his reticent son made it all the more miraculous.

And then, just as I was beginning to enjoy the fantasy, Dan started backpedaling. My enthusiasm unnerved him. "I mean, it's just an idea," he said. "I'm not sure I can do it. I'd have to see if I could run for at least an hour before we told Dad."

We did our first "trial run" during a Burfoot family reunion vacation during 4th of July week. We had traveled to a bucolic state park in West Virginia, and while Amby went for a swim, Dan and I stole away for a secret workout. It was hot, hilly, and hard, but we managed to last for an hour and 20 minutes by alternating four minutes of running and one minute of walking. When we returned to the cabin, Amby asked where we'd been.

"We went for a run," I said.

"You did? It seemed like you were gone a long time. How far did you go?"

I'm a lousy liar. I told him the truth.

"What?" he said. "No, you didn't. What, are you training for Athens?"

"Ha, ha. Yeah, right." I replied.

When we got home, I sent in our race applications. But Dan still didn't feel sure about running the marathon, as he confided to me one afternoon when Amby was at work.

"I don't know," he said. "Maybe I should back out."

"Dan, there's no turning back now. This omelet is cooked," I said.

"I don't know," he repeated. "I need to do a few more training runs to make sure."

"Of course we'll do more training runs. But we're going to Athens."

Jeff Galloway—an Olympian and Amby's college roommate—recommended a strategy for us: Alternate 30 seconds of running and 30 seconds of walking during our training runs and throughout the marathon itself. He suggested using a pedometer-like device called a "GymBoss" that beeped the intervals. Jeff is from Atlanta and has a deep Southern accent. The first time he mentioned the device to me, I thought he called it a "JimBob." The name stuck.

Dan and I wanted to start our training runs well before the worst heat of the day set in, but we couldn't steal away until Amby left for the office. Sometimes Amby worked at home in the mornings and didn't leave until 10:00 a.m. Sure enough, he stuck around all morning the day Dan and I planned our first significant long run, a 16-miler in early August. It was hot and intensely sunny. It took us well over three hours, but we kept it going by arguing politics (Dan: libertarian; me: liberal), reciting poetry (Tennyson's "Ulysses": "To strive, to seek, to find, and not to yield"), and recalling the immortal words of World War I General Ferdinand Foch, which Dan often thought of while struggling through his freshman year at Harvard ("My right is retreating, my center is giving way, situation excellent, I am attacking"). When JimBob beeped, indicating a 30-second run, Dan said, "Attack, attack." When it beeped again for a 30-second walk, he said, "Fall back, fall back."

The long run had gone fairly well, considering the conditions, until we got home and Dan calmly mentioned that his heart was racing. We'd been back for at least 15 minutes, and his heart rate should have returned to normal. Indeed, we were running so moderately, it shouldn't have been elevated much at all.

"Oh my god, Dan," I said. "Do I need to take you to the emergency room?"

"No, no. I'm fine."

I looked him over critically. Dan's mother and I had become friendly over the years. She always greeted me with a big smile and warm hug whenever we saw each other. However, I figured it would put a serious crimp in our relationship if I killed her only son.

"How about I call Nat?"

Dan's aunt Natalie was a psychiatric nurse who'd also been schooled in the workings of the body. Plus, she was smart and cool-headed in these types of situations. And Gary had since let her and Bill in on our secret.

Natalie told me to take Dan's pulse. It was still too high. She asked us some other questions that I don't remember. She pointed out that Dan hadn't undergone a physical and so wasn't cleared for this kind of activity. Dan totally pooh-poohed that, but I'd heard stories of terrifically fit young men who suddenly dropped dead on the basketball court or during cross-country races. I started to panic. Then Natalie uncovered something else that neither Dan nor I had thought of. He had given blood less than 48 hours before this long, hot run. That's causing it, Nat said. She told him to sip fluids and told me to keep checking his pulse and call her back in an hour. Dan headed to his room for a nap. "Fine," I said, "but if you're not up in an hour, I'm coming in to make sure you're not dead."

Dan and I couldn't decide when to surprise Amby with our news about the marathon. We fantasized about Dan taking a separate flight to Athens, staying in a different hotel, and casually lining up next to Amby on the starting line in Marathon. Good fantasy, but too complicated to pull off. Gary came up with a perfect suggestion: Tell him on his birthday. Amby would be turning 64 in mid-August.

We chose to celebrate Amby's birthday at his favorite brew pub. I couldn't even wait for Dan and Amby to order their beer before I nudged the card toward him that announced our news.

"This is from Dan and me," I said, practically bouncing out of my chair. "Happy birthday."

Amby opened the card and read the words but just did not get it. The message couldn't have been clearer; I wrote it in big, bold letters. He just stared at me and then Dan with his mouth open.

"What does this mean?"

Not exactly the reaction I expected.

"What do you mean, 'What does this mean?' It means

we're running the Athens Marathon with you."

It didn't matter what I said. The concept of Dan running a marathon and me running a marathon stretched Amby's concept of reality too far out beyond his known universe — so much so that he just couldn't comprehend it.

"Like, you're running with me in spirit?" he asked.

"No. Like we're running with you in person."

I put my finger under Amby's bearded chin and pushed his mouth closed. Then Dan and I traded off telling him about our long runs (including Dan's brush with cardiac arrest), about entering the race, about Gary stealthily buying Dan a plane ticket. When Amby finally got it, he turned giddy. That was more like it.

A month before the marathon, I spotted a sign at our local farmer's market for the Emmaus Halloween 5-K. The race offered a $100 prize for the best costumed runners. Costumed runners! All I'd been thinking about for months was the Greek warrior Pheidippides. It was just too perfect. I could make a Pheidippides costume for Amby and a companion garment for myself — a Greek goddess, perhaps. But I just couldn't think of myself as a goddess. Instead I'd call myself "Pheidippides' lesser-known girlfriend." We'd be a shoo-in.

My friend Mildred and I finished both costumes just in time for the race. When the starting gun went off, Amby and I (I mean, Pheidippides and his lesser-known girlfriend), plus assorted Sponge Bobs, fuzzy dice, and a family of breakfast items (a pancake, an egg, and a slice of bacon) raced through the streets of Emmaus on a crisp, moonlit evening. Wildly cheering spectators lined the sidewalks, not because Emmaus is full of road-running enthusiasts, but because they had nothing else to do while waiting for the annual Halloween parade to begin.

Amby steamed along effortlessly, while I huffed and

puffed at his side and begged him to slow down. (We were, after all, supposed to be a couple.) He was having entirely too much fun wielding his plastic sword and yelling, "Rejoice! We conquer!" a thousand times. Of course, no one in the crowd knew what he was talking about. They didn't know he was impersonating the great Greek messenger Pheidippides, the original marathoner. Oh no. Instead, they said, "Hey! It's a gladiator!" (Roman) or "Julius Caesar!" (Roman) or "Spartacus!" (Roman).

Whatever. We had a great time, and Amby clearly loved hamming it up. We didn't win the vote for best costume, however, for which I am still bitter. Sponge Bob's family must've stuffed the ballot box. I put away the costumes and figured I'd bring them out again if we ever got invited to a come-as-your-favorite-Greek-historical-figure party. Or if *Sports Illustrated* called.

The following week, *Sports Illustrated* called. A reporter wanted to interview Amby about the Athens Marathon. He would be flying there on assignment to write a story about the anniversary race in particular and the recent marathon boom in general. Amby mentioned the costumes. For reasons I still don't understand, this bit of intelligence fired up the imagination of the reporter.

"Wow, that's great," he told Amby. "Are you going to wear them in the marathon?"

"Uh, no," Amby said.

"Oh, that's too bad," the reporter said.

We thought that was the end of that, but the SI writer called again. He said he'd spoken to his editor about the costumes. If we brought them to Athens, they would take pictures of us, and maybe they'd use the pictures with his story. Amby said, "Sure. We'll bring them."

The day before the marathon, Amby and I once again

donned our Athenian finery. An *SI* photographer posed us on a rocky outcropping overlooking the Acropolis. He took several shots of Amby and me together, but lots more of Amby alone, giving me a chance to admire him. He did look glorious, set against a cloudless blue sky with the brilliant afternoon light glinting off the gold fabric, and the Parthenon gleaming in the distance. I will never forget that moment.

The reporter came to the photo shoot, too. He was an affable guy and seemed to be enjoying every minute.

"You two look great," he said. "Are you sure you don't want to run in your costumes?"

I was sure. But Amby was softening. We'd also been photographed for the *New York Times*. And at the last minute, *Runner's World* sent a photographer to Athens and assigned Amby to write a feature story.

That night he started hinting that he wanted me to run the marathon in my costume, too. Amby never asks me for anything.

"Do you really want me to?" I asked.

"Yeah," he said, sheepishly. "I do."

I sighed.

"Okay."

No matter how many marathons you've run, when you stand on the starting line again, you never know what might happen over the next 26.2 miles. All runners are thrilled that the long-awaited day has finally arrived, but nervous about taking on the long road ahead. On marathon morning, the mixture of excitement and anticipation creates a buzz so strong you can almost touch it. Just before the start, runners everywhere bounce and stretch, tie and retie shoelaces, call out to their friends, recheck their watches.

At the starting area of the Athens Marathon, we breathed in cool fresh air and basked in the brilliant morning light.

Balloons of all colors rose to the sky over the town of Marathon. Festive Greek music blasted from speakers, along with shouts of "Opa!" which one of our guides had told me means, "I am happy and ready to dance." I felt happy and ready to run—and even kind of beautiful, wearing my Greek goddess outfit. At last the starting horn blared and we—12,500 of us—began running 26.2 miles toward the city of Athens.

Amby, Dan, and I, and my brothers-in-law Gary and Bill, clipped right along for the first several miles, as appreciative Greek spectators yelled "Bravo!" They loved Amby's costume and cheered, "Pheidippides!" (finally!) and to me, "Aphrodite!" One spectator handed us olive branches to take to Athens; probably the hero messenger Pheidippides carried one in 490 B.C. It was all so glorious.

Three miles later, I was sitting in a Porta-John. It was your typical Porta-John—dark green, plastic, smelly—the kind you might see at a construction site, an outdoor festival, or, if you're a runner like me, along race courses. I didn't know it at the time, but it was the first of approximately 13 Porta-Johns I would be forced to visit over the next 17 miles or so. With each pit stop, I wrestled with the flowing Greek goddess dress— and the running shorts I wore under the dress—to put my butt onto the seat. I may have looked like a Greek goddess, but I was, in fact, a mortal human being whose mortal human digestive system had chosen this particular day to turn its insides out.

Every time I exited a Porta-John, I was sure I'd be able to start running again. My stomach didn't hurt; I was just suffering from, well, how to say it … exploding butt. My butt felt like it was on fire. I didn't know why; this had never happened to me before.

Gary and Bill left me after my first pit stop. Dan and Amby held out for two more. Then Dan inched ahead as I veered toward another Porta-John. That's when Amby told me they couldn't wait for me anymore.

"I'm sorry," he said.

"It's okay," I said. I wanted him to leave me to battle my rebellious butt alone. Amby and I have been together for decades, but this was not the kind of intimacy I wanted to share with him. Besides, maybe whatever plagued me (the plague?) was contagious. I didn't want him to catch it.

It was a shame, really, and not just for me. Ever since mid-August, Amby had been envisioning us running into the Olympic stadium toward a three-way family finish or, better still, a five-way family finish. That vision was now as dead as the brave Athenian soldiers buried in a mound in Marathon.

At 16 miles or so I tried to run for the umpteenth time. Nope. No way. My butt wouldn't allow it. I saw a coffee shop up ahead on the right. My butt wanted me to go there. My butt thought a coffee shop toilet might be a nice change of scenery from a Porta-John.

I scurried inside, trying to be discreet. I scanned the place, searching for the restroom. The patrons erupted into riotous applause. "Bravo!" they shouted. At me? And then I remembered. Oh yeah. The marathon. I was wearing a Greek goddess outfit. So much for discreet.

I had many more miles to go. Too many. The course didn't offer much scenery — not since Marathon and not until Athens — to distract me. Just billboards and commercial store fronts. I would walk past them, try to jog, my butt would say, "Oh no you don't," and I would walk again. And wonder when I'd find the next Porta-John, which had become like little roadside shrines for me.

On and on I walked. The sun was intense and getting hotter. The road stretched out before me, shimmering like a scene in a creepy movie. I could feel my face getting sunburned, and my right foot hurt. I stopped to take off my shoe and adjust the tongue, which had been cutting into the front of my ankle. I saw that one of my toenails was turning black and then … my butt—no way—started to complain again. I wondered, how much can one person possibly purge?

Then, as I continued my slow trek toward Athens, wondering whether I would get there before sunset, an angel stopped by. She was tall and broad and wearing a white cap adorned with wings. I wasn't hallucinating, but after what I'd been through the last several hours, it wasn't entirely improbable. The angel was Jennifer, a member of our larger touring group and a leader of Team In Training, a group of marathoners who raise money for cancer research. She was running so strong and looked so fresh that I wondered why she was so far back. She explained that she'd been running up and down the course all day, checking on members of her group.

"What are you doing back here?" she asked.

I told her how my butt had hijacked me.

"Do you have any salt?"

"No," I said. But I could certainly pick up some at the next coffee shop.

"I do." Jennifer reached into her enormous belt pack. She appeared to have an entire drugstore strapped around her waist.

"Here," she said, pouring about half a teaspoon into my hand. "You'll feel better soon, I promise." She gave me a drink from her water bottle to wash it down.

"Thanks," I said.

"See you at the finish line."

"I hope so."

Then Jennifer flew away as suddenly as she appeared.

I didn't really believe the salt would cure me. But, in a half-mile or so, I tried to jog, and I felt okay. Then better than okay. I picked up the pace. Still good. It was a miracle. And my legs weren't even tired—not after so much walking (and sitting). I'd been out on the road to Athens for almost six hours and had a little over three miles to go. I ran faster. I didn't even care if I flamed out before I reached the finish line. I felt too good to go slow.

I flew past the mammoth glass sculpture of a marathon runner at the 25-mile mark. I still couldn't see the stadium. But I was getting close, I knew, because I saw balloon arches forming a canopy over the street.

Then I beheld a most welcome sight, more beautiful than the finish line even: the gleaming gold figure of my Pheidippides, smiling broadly, his arms open wide. Amby looked thrilled to see me, obviously relieved that I hadn't been forced to drop out. I was expecting Amby to be there, of course, because he always waited for me at every race. He didn't even have to stay on the sidelines this time; the course had emptied out, so he could stand in the middle of the road to greet me. But Dan, too? I didn't expect to see him. I figured he must've felt really great after crossing the finish line if he still had the energy to walk back and cheer for me. Every time I'd finished a marathon I just wanted to lie down as soon as possible.

I blew Amby kisses and waved gaily to Dan. Then Amby shouted something peculiar: "You have to slow down!"

Whatever for? Did he think I was going to hurt myself? I yelled back: "I'm fine! I don't want to break my stride!" and hauled full bore into the stadium. Fifty yards from the finish line, I heard Gary and Bill. "Go Cristina!" they shouted and clapped. I waved at them and at the spectators, the few who were left, seated in the marble stands. I crossed the finish line in over six hours. But I didn't care about the time. I did it. I survived.

Right away I saw Jennifer, the running angel. I gave her a big hug and thanked her, feeling so grateful that I started to cry. I found my sister-in-law, hugged her, too, and shed a few

116

more tears.

"Congratulations, Cristina," Natalie said. "Here comes Amby and Dan!" She pointed and I saw them walking toward me on the track.

I was amazed that they had made their way back into the stadium so quickly from where I last saw them. They both hugged me and then Amby asked me something truly perplexing: "Why did you pass us outside the stadium?"

"Why did I pass you? What are you talking about?"

"You passed us outside the stadium," he said. "We were supposed to finish together."

"What? But you were already finished."

After much discussion we sorted out what happened. At the 20-mile mark, Dan "hit the wall," his legs hurting so badly that they started to cramp. His 30-second walk breaks grew longer. Finally he gave up running altogether. Amby stayed with him as they walked—a slow, slow Dan-style walk—the final three miles. I didn't know it, but that's when I started catching them. When I saw them outside the stadium, I assumed they'd already crossed the finish line, so I blew past them without a second thought.

Amby had said to Dan, "What just happened?"

"Maybe she's mad at you for leaving her behind," Dan theorized. "You're in trouble now."

But none of that mattered. We were all together now, my family and me, in this glorious historic stadium, a monument to victory. And we had yet another funny story to add to our pantheon of funny family stories. My macho stepson provided the punch line. He refused to admit that he'd been crippled by the marathon distance. He claimed that leaving me behind to suffer alone had caused him psychological stress and slowed him down. "We were handicapped by guilt," he said. That's my Dan.

Cristina Negrón is a freelance editor and writer who has completed 13 marathons. "Rejoice! We Conquer!" is an excerpt from Cristina's 2013 memoir, So Far.

The 27th Mile

Joggling Red Rock Canyon

by Perry Romanowski

"I believe there is no God."

This phrase was echoing in my head while I passed the 22nd mile marker during the 2009 Red Rock Canyon marathon. It was put there by Penn Jillette with a little help from Steve Jobs (iPod), Nathaniel Baldwin (headphones), and Jay Allison, the editor of the excellent audio book *This I Believe* from which Jillette was reading. The words startled me like the sound of an 18-wheeler truck horn unexpectedly blaring behind me. All sensations stopped and my attention fixated on the sounds that entered my skull through my right ear:

> I'm not greedy. I have love, blue skies, rainbows and Hallmark cards, and that has to be enough. It has to be enough, but it's everything in the world and everything in the world is plenty for me. It seems just rude to beg the invisible for more. Just the love of my family that raised me and the family I'm raising now is enough that I don't need heaven. I won the huge genetic lottery and I get joy every day.

As I listened, I looked around at the gorgeous scenery. Gigantic colored rocks reached up to a near-cloudless blue sky. A sea of chalky dirt and rocks surrounded me. It was speckled with dried bushes and desert shrubs that looked like lifeless sea anemones. In the distance, three deer navigated the terrain, oblivious to passing cars, marathon runners and questions about creation.

"Could this really be all there is?" I wondered. "Is this heaven?"

Moments like these are common in later marathon miles.

121

They are usually prompted by some unexpected sight, sound or feeling that shakes your endorphin-clouded mind and gives you a brief flash of clarity. Stabbing muscle pains, joint soreness, and chafing sting momentarily disappear, replaced with intense focus on a single thought. Sometimes the thought is about existence and your place in the universe. But more often the thought is, "Why the hell am I doing this!?"

These negative thoughts plagued me sooner in this canyon marathon than in most previous marathons. They started around mile 4 while I ran next to a 42-year-old, first-time marathoner named Troy. He saw me joggling and was interested in learning more about it.

You see, I'm a joggler. I juggle while I run. I started joggling back in 1996 as a way to make running more interesting, and I've done it ever since.

I answered Troy's questions and asked him a few about himself. We went on to talk about the canyon, Las Vegas, his training, our race expectations, and other bits of life's minutiae.

"Are you going to keep this pace up the whole way?" he asked.

"I'm going to try to," I replied.

"Good. Me too."

As we scaled the 1000-foot incline, I looked down to adjust my headphone cord and my sunglasses fell to the ground and broke. A voice said, "I don't know why you keep running these stupid races." I glared at my running companion then realized it wasn't him but my homunculus, the little voice inside my head, who said it. "Just ignore him," I thought. "Don't think, just keep joggling."

Troy was nice enough to stop with me and hold my juggling bags while I tried to fix my glasses. I couldn't repair them, so I shoved them in my back pocket, took back my Gballz (juggling balls), pulled down the bill of my Nike hat, and resumed joggling. As I steadily pulled away from Troy, the negative voice in my head returned. I turned on my audio book and let the melodious words of Studs Terkel drown him out. The fifth mile of a marathon is no place for negativity.

The course of the Red Rock Canyon marathon is roughly a U-shaped, 13-mile winding road. You start at about 3700 feet elevation and build to 4700 feet in the first 5 miles. It flattens for a couple of miles and then it descends from mile 9 through 13 back to 3700 ft. At the half-way point, you turn around and go back to where you started. All the downhills you loved on the way there become grueling uphills on the way back. If you're not used to running hills, it's rough.

I managed to focus on the various voices of the *This I Believe* book and steadily cruised through the first half. Except for a couple miles where I played rabbit and tortoise with a faster runner who kept stopping to take pictures (he was the rabbit), I ran alone after I left Troy behind.

There was no cheering crowd to amuse with joggling tricks. No rock bands or DJs to get my blood pumping. For miles, there was only me, my audio books, flying Gballz, and the isolation of the canyon desert.

I heard different authors in my ear, catching phrases like "I believe in God" or "There is no job more important than parenting", but their words were steadily reduced to a low tinnitus-like hum in my head. Sadness and loneliness engulfed me like a cloud. Only the instinct to finish kept me joggling and moving forward.

Around mile 10, my mood brightened upon seeing runners coming from the other direction. These were the half-marathon runners who had started a little over an hour and a half after us. They cheered and yelled as they passed by, things like "Way to go juggler!" "You're incredible!" "Oh my God! That's great!" I was reinvigorated.

Every couple of miles, there were roadside tables manned

by two or three volunteers. They handed out life-saving water, sport drinks, and cookies that propelled you into the next mile. More importantly, they cheered enthusiastically. They made me feel like a Hot Wheels car going through an accelerator box. At mile 12 there was one lady handing out water with her three kids. Their faces lit up when they saw me joggling.

"That's so cool!" one of them yelled.

I grinned from ear to ear. While passing I turned around and did a little backwards joggling. They cheered louder and it pushed me to go faster.

At the turn-around, I saw the steepness of the hill I had just ascended. Going back up was not appealing. I kept reminding myself that the last five miles would be an easy downhill. That worked right up through mile 16 when I gave in to my pain and walked up a steep incline.

Thankfully, I've practiced juggling while walking (walggling?) so it was easy to keep the pattern going. Throughout the rest of the race I walked intermittently whenever the hills got too steep. It certainly added about 15 minutes to my time. But it also ensured that I would finish.

In mile 22, I was alone again and feeling deliriously tired when those words of Penn Jillette woke me up. "I believe there is no God."

I listened intently when he said:

Believing there's no God means I can't really be forgiven except by kindness and faulty memories. That's good; it makes me want to be more thoughtful. I have to try to treat people right the first time around.

And when he finished by saying that belief in no God "…encourages me to make this life the best life I will ever have."

His words kept me pondering for the remaining miles. Sure, I noticed each mile marker and the few other runners that I passed, but they only briefly disturbed my storming thoughts. What did I believe?

I didn't come to any final conclusions but I thought the following:

This world, this canyon, this race, this moment is all there is. Life provides no after-race snacks of cookies, bagels, nachos and hot chicken soup as there were after this marathon. Life's finish line does not have a timing mat that tells you that you finished in 4:07:44 (24th place out of 125 finishers).

This life is all you get. You succeed and fail through your hard work, your efforts and sometimes with help from cosmic luck. Whether this luck is God, I can't really say. I doubt it.

But I can say I believe in this life. I believe in the joy of joggling. And I believe that marathons can push your body and mind in ways you wouldn't think possible.

Perry Romanowski has been running for over twenty years. In 1996, he began to juggle while he ran. These days, he joggles through every workout and race. Perry completed his 34th marathon in 2013, and he owns a personal best of 3:21. He is also a streak runner who has joggled at least 1.5 miles every day since November 18, 2008. "Joggling Red Rock Canyon" originally appeared on his blog, justyouraveragejoggler.com.

I Had to Pee

by Lawrence Block

I had to pee.

Well, that was only to be expected. I'd made my usual trips through the PortaJohn line at the marathon's staging ground, but I'd walked several miles since then, and it was time to answer nature's call. That could be awkward in a race through the crowded streets of a large city, but there was really nothing to it when you were out in the country. And we were on the outskirts of Anchorage, racing along an asphalt path through parkland that was pretty close to wilderness. Take a dozen steps off the pavement, and the only witness to your peeing would be the songbirds and the rabbits.

And the moose, and the bears — and that was the problem, because a dozen steps was farther from the path than it was advisable to be. The woods began perhaps half that many steps away, and one really didn't want to be an uninvited guest at the Teddy Bears' Picnic.

At Athens the previous year — that's in Ohio, not Greece — we'd been on a similar path through parkland, and it had been a small enough race so that privacy was never an issue. There just weren't that many others in the race, and they were all out in front of me. And the slow ones were too busy contending with the course to pay attention to an old guy watering the flowers.

Not so in Anchorage.

For several years, the Mayor's Midnight Sun Marathon had drawn great quantities of America's slowest runners, and some of them couldn't properly be described as runners at all. Almost six hundred men and eight hundred women completed the race, and a substantial proportion of them were running it as a part of Team In Training, a national organization raising funds to combat leukemia and lymphoma—and I have to say its purpose was as laudable as its acronym was unfortunate. All of the Team In Training entrants were decked out in purple shirts, and the staging area before the start was an ocean of purple. There were entrants from every state, except for West Virginia. I don't know what happened to West Virginia.

For most of the Purple People, this was a first marathon, and the race organizers went out of their way to encourage first-timers, keeping the finish line open for a very generous eight and a half hours. It is always a challenge to complete a marathon, but it is rather less formidable a challenge when you've got eight and a half hours available to you. You can still go all out, of course, but you don't have to. You can relax. You can slow down. You can take time to sprinkle the flowers, or even to smell them.

The ranks of the Purple People included more than a handful of flower-smellers. Some of them had binoculars around their necks, so that they could get a good look at the flowers—or, if they were lucky (or unlucky, depending on the outcome), at the moose and bears. More had cameras, and stopped occasionally to take pictures of the glorious landscape, or, less gloriously, of each other. They were in no hurry, many of these purple-clad warriors, and what was wrong with that? They were exerting themselves in a good cause, and when it was all over they'd have finished a marathon.

So there I was, a step or two off the path, facing away from the stream of runners flowing slowly behind me, and staring vaguely off into the distance. And a cheerful young woman in a purple T-shirt interrupted her running to hurry over and position herself next to me, eager to find out what was commanding my attention.

"Hi," she said. "Are you looking at something

wonderful?"

You can imagine the several responses I considered and rejected. What I said, sternly, I'm afraid, was, "Go away." And she did. And, a moment later, so did I.

Lawrence Block's most recent novels are Hit Me, *featuring Keller, and* A Drop of the Hard Stuff, *featuring Matthew Scudder, who will be played by Liam Neeson in the forthcoming film,* A Walk Among the Tombstones. *Several of his other books have been filmed, although not terribly well. For more, visit lawrenceblock.wordpress.com. "I Had to Pee" is an excerpt from his book,* Step by Step.

Rage, Rage

by Jason Fisk

I remember hiking a mountain with my sister Abby and looking out over the city of Tucson from the top, absorbing the dry desert beauty.

Growing up, Abby became my best friend by default. We never lived in one house for more than three years; she was someone who was always there for me. The fact that she was a tomboy made it that much easier for me to relate to her.

She had such an adventurous spirit. She was super competitive too. One time, when all of the neighbor kids had gathered around our front stoop to watch me eat a live worm, she stole my thunder by popping one into her mouth and eating it before I had even worked up the nerve to put it anywhere near my lips. I eventually stopped playing board games with her because she was so competitive.

The trip down the mountain path went twice as fast as the hike to the top had taken. I loved how the pull of gravity forced my mind to act quickly, sending messages to my feet: jump, quick, turn, slow down, speed up, turn, jump, catch yourself. Near the bottom, Abby turned to me and said, "Isn't this a rush?"

"It is," I said, "but do you wanna know what's an even bigger rush?"

"What," she said, dabbing the sweat from her forehead.

"Running a marathon, and finally crossing the finish line."

I had just run the Chicago Marathon two months before. I told Abby about running over that last incline, rounding the final corner, and seeing the finish line right there before me. I told her about the beauty of complete strangers cheering for me, acknowledging all the hard work I had put into training, cheering for all of the miles I had logged over the past four months. And I told her about the strange combination of exhilaration, exhaustion, and adrenalin that coursed through my being as they draped the Mylar blanket over my shoulders, cut the timing chip from my shoe, and handed me the heavy finishers' medal.

"So, how about it?" I asked her at the foot of the trail.

"You want to run a marathon with me?" she asked.

"Yes. It's ten times the rush this was. Come on."

Eventually, she acquiesced, and we began our long-distance training together. She was in Tucson, and I was in Chicago. We called each other before, and after, our long runs. We encouraged each other daily with e-mails and phone calls. We ran through the pain and complained about the whole process together. We questioned the sanity of the long runs, and were in awe at how much time training was taking from everything else in our lives, specifically our spouses. It felt as if the training had taken over my life, and the race would never happen. It wasn't until I picked her up at the airport that I realized we would be running the marathon in just a matter of days.

Race morning came, and I remember standing there with Abby in the middle of tens of thousands of people, feeling their energy, sharing the moment. The music was being pumped from loudspeakers everywhere. There was a helicopter flying above the crowd, filming for the news. Then there was an announcement, and then the BANG of the start gun. As we looked out over the crowd, we saw hundreds of warm-up shirts being tossed to the side of the road, and we jogged in place as we waited for our turn to get to the start line.

We ran. We absorbed Chicago as we ran through the neighborhoods: The Loop, Boystown, Chinatown, and the rest. We didn't talk a lot. Occasionally, we'd point to this or that, and nod, or ask, "Isn't this cool?"

It was at mile marker 23 that we both began to run out of fuel, or hit the wall, as they say. We had been out of sync for most of the run, trying to find the other's pace, and we were now paying for that extra effort.

At one point we stopped to walk, and a stocky man came up behind me and pushed me forward. "Keep going," he said. We ran again, and eventually, slowly, covered the last three miles. We came up over the hill, rounded the corner, and ran toward the finish line. It was as if we were in slow motion, heavy feet plodding toward our goal. We crossed the finish line together, hugged, and then we both started crying.

I found myself crying in her presence again six years later. I walked into the hospital room and saw her sitting in the bed with her bony knees covered by sterile white blankets. I saw how her face had sunk into itself, and her collarbones and shoulders were more pronounced, exaggerated, from all of her weight loss, and I had to turn away to collect myself and wipe away the tears.

To sum up her three-year battle with ulcerative colitis, she lost her colon, lost her daughter in utero, and was now struggling with a horribly painful abscess surrounding the area where the ileostomy emptied waste into a plastic bag hanging from her side. She was having a difficult time eating, let alone processing food. She was only 36 years old, much too young to be dealing with any of this. Instantly, I thought of Dylan Thomas's poem "Do Not Go Gentle Into That Good Night," and I wanted her to, "Rage, rage against the dying of the light."

Shortly after I arrived, Abby complained of a headache, the nurse gave her a painkiller, and she fell asleep. I relieved my brother-in-law from his bedside watch, and gave him a much-needed break. He went back to the hotel to take a nap. I sat by her side and read for three hours while she passed away. Her headache had not been a migraine, but a stroke. Abby never woke up again.

I have run 1,714 miles since her death. I know this because I started keeping track the day I came back home from Rochester. I would get out there on the forest preserve paths and run and run. I saw her in the shadows as I ran through the woods. I would see her in my peripheral vision as I rounded corners. I loved running there because I felt close to her. I still love running there, and feel as if I've made a sort of supernatural bond with the woods. I think my sister visits me there, and follows me as I run.

I had many questions that I needed answers to as I ran and ran and ran. One of the biggest was, did she "Rage against the dying of the light"? She had such a difficult time eating food and … I wondered, on occasion, if there was a point where she had just given up the fight. There were phone calls where we had talked, and she had expressed a dejected, almost fatalistic attitude toward the whole process. Add to that the fact that she was hardly eating near the end, and she had withered away physically, and it raised questions for me. There were times when the doctors had to prescribe intravenous nutrition to give her the nourishment she needed to stay alive. I questioned whether or not she had given up. It was eating at my heart and soul. I had so wanted her to RAGE! and wasn't convinced that she had.

One day, after she had passed away, her husband called, and I shared with him my doubts about her fighting, and asked out loud if he thought she had given up or not. I needed reassurance that she had not gone without a fight. He then told me that she had taken her Chicago Marathon medal with her to the Mayo Clinic and had it sitting next to her on the bedside stand the whole time she was there. At that moment, I knew that she had worked as hard to stay alive as she and I had worked to run those 26.2 miles. And on my run that day,

134

in the woods, I felt her there, and knew that the third time I cried in her presence was a celebration of her and the fight she had put up against ulcerative colitis. She had most certainly raged against the dying of the light.

Jason Fisk is a husband, a father of two, and a teacher who lives in the suburbs of Chicago. He is the author of short- (and shorter-) story collections Hank and Jules *and* Salt Creek Anthology, *and* the fierce crackle of fragile wings, *a book of poetry, as well as two poetry chapbooks,* The Sagging: Spirits *and* Skin and Decay. *For more, visit www.JasonFisk.com. "Rage, Rage" is an original piece for* The 27th Mile.

On the Run from Dogs and People

by Hal Higdon

It is harder to explain a marathon than to run one. I rediscover this each year as I get ready for the Boston Marathon, which is to American road runners what the Masters is to golfers, or what Wimbledon used to be to tennis players. And I realize anew, almost with the startling suddenness of a crocus or snowdrop announcing spring's verdant competitions, that, much as I love my sport, it is somewhat weird. Who but an idiot would race 26 tortured miles plus 385 yards for the dubious distinction of finishing 38th? Well, a scholar would. Of the 200 or so runners who will be at the starting line at noon on April 19 (which is Patriots Day, a holiday in Massachusetts), about 25 will have won their Master's or Doctor's degree.

The Boston Marathon is relentlessly amateur. No one gets anything but glory from the race – and who is responsible for keeping it pure? A professional sports figure – Walter Brown, owner of the Boston Bruins and Celtics – and his father before him have been carrying the race for 50 years, unchanged and uncommercialized.

I said glory. Glory? I exaggerate. A third of a million politely applauding New Englanders will line the course and the race will be reported in Boston and throughout the rest of the world except, of course, in the U.S., where a junior high potato-sack race commands more editorial attention.

The list of paradoxes in distance running is long. It is reasonable, I suppose, that Americans should be amused by the sport. I am not sure, however, that most of his fellowmen should consider it their bounden duty to taunt the road racer whenever he trots over the horizon. They do, though, and the distance runner in America has become almost inured to the

137

kidding, gentle or otherwise, that he has had to endure in piling up hundreds and even thousands of miles in training in order to compete successfully in a race like the Boston Marathon. Let the marathon runner clad in sweat clothes step out onto a golf course or a park sidewalk, and some comedian will roll down a car window to shout an Army cadence: "Hup, two, three, four." This is a hilarious joke, at least as funny as the one that breaks up photographers: "Her face will break your camera."

The runner plods on. People turn to stare and children, who have a legitimate reason for being in the park without golf club in hand, ask questions: "Hey, you a runner?" No, I'm a well-conditioned purse-snatcher, you think, but you answer respectfully. "Are you training for that track meet?" asks another (meaning the Pan American Games), and you answer, yes, even though you are not good enough to make the team.

"Are youse guys boxers?" a couple of tough-looking slum broads asked Lawton Lamb and me once as we ran together in Chicago's Washington Park. (You would be amazed—or would you?—at the number of people who consider it more worthy to train for a fight than a road race.) Sure, we replied, afraid they might smash us if we admitted being only trackmen. Lately a new question has been added: "Hey, you running 50 miles?" The New Frontier has made even the marathon almost respectable.

Occasionally you do run into a comment that is actually funny. Ted Corbitt, a distance man from the Bronx, runs to the subway on his way to work as part of his training program. One day a guy said to his friend as Corbitt jogged by, "Man, that cat's late every morning."

Long-distance runners don't fear children or even slum broads, because their teeth aren't sharp—at least, not very sharp. Dogs are another matter. "Only two things bother me when I'm running in Central Park," New York's Peter

138

McArdle once told me. "Dogs and policemen." I don't know about policemen, but at one point or another all marathoners come to hate dogs—especially big, sleek, fast dogs. Dogs distrust anyone who has two legs and runs. They reason, perhaps like their masters, that the runner must be fleeing from someone or something. They're right, too—he's escaping the dogs.

While in the Army and training over in Germany one year, a German shepherd dog chomped through three layers of clothing and put me out of commission for a week. He came padding up behind me, his tail wagging, and I suspected nothing sinister until he struck. After his teeth sank in I knew how the French had felt about Alsace-Lorraine. Back in Chicago a few years later, another dog ran a good 200 yards across a park lawn to knock me down, thereby twisting my knee. He could have finished me off if he had been hungry. I was in the 14th mile of a hard workout and in no mood to bite back. Still another hound chased over the frozen ice of a pond one winter with my behind in his sights, but I thwarted him by climbing a children's slide. I must have looked heroic. Fred Wilt used to carry a club in one hand while running through the park to beat off dogs (and presumably policemen), but I'm not as aggressive as Fred. Maybe that's why I never made an Olympic team. Nowadays when I sniff dog flesh I retreat in the other direction.

Another more insidious hazard is the cocktail party—not the cocktails, but the people who drink them. "Don't tell me you're still running," chortles the husband of a schoolmate of my wife while munching on hors d'oeuvres.

"Don't tell me you're still feeding your gut," I think, but don't say so, because I possess more tact than courage.

Almost as dangerous is the old friend who has long since accepted your hobby but in a gathering of strangers forgets that others may not possess an equally liberal mind. "I saw you running in the park the other night," he says with a friendly smile.

Clear across the room it is as though the strap holding Jayne Mansfield's evening gown had just snapped. "My husband runs the marathon," my wife explains. She might just as well have told them I was a Buddhist priest. A dozen tongues click and the women look with sympathy at my wife. Having a husband who is a marathon runner seems infinitely worse than one who is an alcoholic or a mere adulterer.

After facing the menacing fangs of dogs in the parks and the equally menacing fangs of Martini sippers at parties, it thus comes as quite a relief to the runner to be able to shed his clothes and compete in a race where, if not adjudged completely insane, he at least is considered only moderately odd. Such a race is the marathon.

The race owes its existence to a Greek courier named Pheidippides, who in 490 B.C. ran from the plains of Marathon to Athens to announce the Athenian victory over an invading Persian army. "Rejoice, we conquer," he gasped, dropping dead and thereby doing irreparable damage to the Greek image of physical fitness. With the Olympic revival in 1896, a Greek shepherd named Spiridon Louis wandered down out of the hills to win the gold medal in a race following the approximate path of Pheidippides.

But neither Pheidippides nor Louis ran the present distance of the marathon. Poor out-of-shape Pheidippides covered a mere 22 miles and 1,500 yards and Louis' route was about 25 miles. When the Olympics came to London in 1908, the British moved the starting line back to Windsor Castle so the royal family could watch the start of the race from their royal balcony. Windsor Castle just happened to be 26 miles and 385 yards away from where the race would end in the Olympic stadium. Britain no longer sets the standards for the world, but on this point she prevailed. Now, whenever a present-day marathoner slogs footsore past the 25-mile mark he always mutters under his breath, "God save the Queen" (or words to that effect).

Impressed with the 1896 Olympic race, Boston Athletic Association Team Manager John Graham imported the marathon to the U.S. in the following year. Fifteen runners appeared at the start, and any distance runner in this country who has ever amounted to anything has either consciously or subconsciously yearned to come home first in Boston ever since.

What can attract so large a group of intelligent men to so materially unrewarding an experience? (The modest prizes include trophies for the first 10 finishers and medals for the next 25.) John Gray, a schoolteacher from Walpole, Mass., sent out a questionnaire to 100 runners and received 66 replies. Among other things he discovered that the average marathoner had run about 2,000 miles the past year. The lowest total reported was 230 miles, the highest Mike O'Hara's 5,100. The average respondent had raced the full marathon distance 14 times, five of them in Boston. O'Hara finished 100 races, a record. On the average, the marathoner was 32 years old, figured he would run for another 19 years, with Nat Cirulnick stating flatly, "I intend to compete for 58 more years, until I'm 90."

Statistics don't mean much, of course. The runner's own words express the real appeal of marathoning better. Dr. Leon Kruger, a 41-year-old pediatrician and a far-back finisher in Boston, told Gray, "Running makes me feel different from men who don't run. I'm more conscious of living rather than just existing."

Sam Ouelette, a 58-year-old janitor from Maine, has finished in Boston 18 times and has three sons who have finished a total of 13 times in a great demonstration of marathoning togetherness. Sam says, "I've never been told I was too old or not good enough, like they say in team sports. If a person wants to stay young, compete the year round."

Pete Bjarkman, a University of Hartford honor student, writes, "As I was dressing for the marathon, I tried to think of any other sport in which a beginner could find himself dressing alongside the world's leading performers."

Don Fay, a young executive, advises aspiring runners, "Don't be afraid of public opinion. Most adverse comment is just jealousy anyway."

Tom Osier, a graduate math student at NYU, says, "Writers should not describe marathoners as 'a clan of masochistic idiots.' A well-trained runner experiences very little pain, even during an all-out effort."

Ken Joseph, a 40-year-old MIT alumnus and a marathoning buddy of Gray's, says, "I even enjoy shoveling snow now that I've started running again. I know I'm not going to drop dead, and I can laugh at the fellows in the office with their gimmicky $150 snow blowers."

And then there was Clarence DeMar. Mr. DeMarathon, somebody once called him, and the punster should be forgiven his trespass for DeMar was wonderful. A seven-time winner of the Boston Marathon, starting in 1911, he was still in the first 10 in the '30s, 17th in 1943, and even in the '50s a young runner had to train thousands of miles to beat him. DeMar ran races right up to within a year of his death at 70 (from cancer, not from the "bad heart" he was told he had in 1912).

DeMar's great tradition, including that of pleasing the crowd, is carried on by Old John Kelley. The safest bet about the Boston Marathon is that, whoever wins the race, John will receive and deserve far greater applause. Now 55, Kelley— who was running this race in the late '20s—needs only a hot day on April 19th to be a real threat for the first 10. Last year in cold weather he was only 25th, but a month later in the

142

national championship in Yonkers he came up with the least recognized performance of the year in any sport when he finished a brilliant fourth in a strong field of 80. A younger runner, expected to be a future champion, matched strides with Kelley for 25 miles over the hilly and extremely demanding course, then staggered to the curb, embraced a telephone pole and nearly collapsed. The old man sped swiftly on — at about 5:15 per mile, a pace that most untrained young men would have trouble keeping for even half a mile.

The youthfulness and the accompanying joy in life of the marathoner is one of the charms of his sport. For once the spectator sees man scoring a victory over Father Time. A temporary victory, admittedly, but a highly dramatic one nevertheless. Where else can you watch an athlete who is better today than he was in 1928 as a 20-year old?

At one time most of the competitors in the Boston Marathon were local products. Today they come from almost anywhere on earth, from such diverse places as Guatemala, Japan, Finland, Ethiopia and Little Rock, Arkansas. Many of these out-of-towners stay at the Hotel Lenox, a middle-aged mausoleum that, since the old athletic club across the street gave way to urban renewal a few years ago, has become both the headquarters of the race and a place of solace for those who go the distance. In front of the Lenox a yellow line has been painted on the street with the word "finish" written behind it. Since only once in the past 17 years has a native-born American won the Boston Marathon, the yellow line in effect has been deeded to foreign runners — such as Finland's Eino Oksanen, Paavo Kotila and Veikko Karvonen, who have won in the past, and Ethiopia's Abebe Bikila, the 1960 Olympic champion, who is entered this year. Abebe has never lost a marathon.

No one can claim to have really eaten breakfast until he has broken fast in the coffee shop of the Hotel Lenox on the morning of the Boston Marathon. The committee on food faddism of the American Medical Association should someday look into what goes on there. Runners sit around grouchily at booths and tables sprinkling sunflower seeds into their oatmeal, swigging wheat germ and sipping Sustagen, the kind of nourishment they give to old ladies dying in the hospital. All year long waitresses at the Lenox get standard orders for waffles and coffee. Come the day of the Boston Marathon, however, and the dialogue goes something like this:

"What would you like for breakfast, sir?"

"Two salt tablets and a glass of orange juice."

But the Lenox waitresses apparently are attuned to the whims of road runners. Two minutes later one will appear with the orange juice and two pills on a silver platter: "Do you want them mixed, sir?"

There is a ritual to the pre-race preparations that is every bit as unusual as the race itself. It begins with a bus ride on the morning of the big day. The better runners usually get chaperoned in cars and by friends to the starting line 26 miles away in Hopkinton, but the rank and file—those who will be lucky to go the distance in three hours—usually take the bus that leaves from in front of the Lenox at 8:30 in the morning. The sponsoring Boston Athletic Association hires one or two shock-absorberless machines that on normal days do nothing more exciting than carry lunch-clutching children to their local grammar school. On Patriots Day these buses take on an extra aura of glamour—and the dank smell of sweat. Runners board the bus clad in street clothes, in warm-up suits and sometimes in nothing more than the shirt and shorts they will wear from start to finish. Not burdened with the nervousness of those who run for records, the road runners converse freely about the race to come and all past marathon races in which they have competed. Some have been riding the bus from the Lenox to Hopkinton for years.

"Remember Tarzan Brown?" chuckles one oldtimer, recalling the Rhode Island Indian who won the Boston Marathon twice, in 1936 and 1939. Others nod in instant recognition. "Back in 1937 it was so hot he went for a swim in Lake Cochituate. It felt so good he decided not to get out." The oldtimers laugh at the familiar story, as though acting out a part in some passion play. In the back of the bus newcomers sit in awed silence.

Someone tells the story of Tom Longboat, an Onondaga Indian from Ontario, who in 1907 surprised the other runners by suddenly springing ahead early in the race. He arrived at a railroad crossing just ahead of a long freight train. It delayed his opponents long enough to guarantee his easy victory — if there ever is easy victory in the marathon. "At the Yonkers Marathon years ago," an anecdotist informs the crowd, "they used to run the last lap around the racetrack. The race starts at noon, you know. They close the track up, and along about 10 or 12 that night this member of the Yonkers Fire Department shows up still trotting. He had to climb over the fence to finish. He had a bet with his buddies."

The marathoners continue to dwell on late finishers: "Ted Vogel came running onto the track in the 1948 Olympic marathon just as they were presenting the awards. The national anthem of the winner's country was playing. Instead of continuing running, he stops on the track and stands at attention."

"That's what I call sportsmanship," volunteered one.

"Yeah?" said a cynic in the crowd. "How many other runners passed him?"

Some on the bus seem much concerned with the problems of being an also-ran. Cars are barred from the entire length of the Boston Marathon course during the race — at least as far as the front runners know. By the time most of those in the bus approach the finish line they will be threading through thick holiday traffic on Commonwealth Avenue. "I don't mind the traffic," says one marathoner. "The discouraging thing is when you get to the 15-mile mark and see a newsboy standing on the corner with the name of the winner in headlines."

About 45 minutes after leaving the Hotel Lenox, the marathoners' bus chugs past Marathon Farm and Marathon Rock. In years past, America's most prestigious road race used to start by this rock, second in New England historical importance only to Plymouth Rock. Foreign track statisticians, however, used to sneer at the fast times turned in on the Boston course—times that used to be entered in the record book of world athletics with an asterisk, like Roger Maris' 61st home run. "The course is short," snorted the foreigners.

"No," answered the sponsoring BAA. "The fast times are in part due to the prevailing wind that usually pushes the runners from behind."

"The course is short," countered the foreigners.

"Not necessarily," insisted the BAA. "Our course is a bit hilly. Since we run toward the sea, it is more downhill than up."

"The course is short," reiterated the foreigners, sounding like a well-worn 78-rpm record. About half a dozen years ago, to still their critics, BAA officials walked out to Hopkinton, tape measures in hand, and remeasured their course. "The course is short," they admitted, their Yankee pride disintegrating. Mumbling something about expressway construction, they moved the starting line half a mile back from fabled Marathon Rock to a nondescript place in the middle of the highway where there isn't even a gas station.

Marathoners must report for a physical at 10 at the Hopkinton high school gym. The bus from the Lenox arrives a little before that hour. Soon the gym bursts with athletes in various states of dress and undress, rubbing liniment into their legs, taping toes to prevent blisters and socializing with all the amiability of delegates at a Lions convention. But nobody at a respectable Lions convention would be caught drinking honey.

The physical itself consists of stepping on a scale, having your heart listened to and pulse taken by a physician. It is the kind of examination that might catch a person in the advanced stages of coronary thrombosis. Yet a certain small number of otherwise sound athletes possess heart murmurs bearing no relationship either to their training or to their health but which cause them to live in constant fear of disqualification. In 1957 the examining doctors thumbed three runners out of the race, including Ted Corbitt, who was a member of the 1952 Olympic team, and Al Confalone, a 1959 U.S. Pan American Games entrant. They ran the race without numbers anyway and finished in the top 10. All survived the experience. Little things such as this cause the marathon runner to distrust medical expertise.

But the ritual proceeds. Having finished with the physical exam, the competitors dress in their running uniforms, pinning numbers front and back, then place their street clothes in a truck that will transport the clothes to the finish line. This provides an incentive to finish, since if they don't get to the finish line one way or another the runners have little chance of getting their clothes back. Marathoners then crowd back into the bus to be transported the half mile to the starting line. Some intrepid competitors who actually expect to finish jog to the start for a warmup, which seems like adding insult to injury.

At this point, most runners, if they have not already done so back in the gym, follow the call of nature. I always jog a couple of hundred yards down the highway to a gas station, which if not included in the current edition of "Where to Go and What to Do in Hopkinton" should be. Usually an amiable gas station attendant directs me and others around the corner, past a grease rack and to a back room. He doesn't know any of our names, I am sure, but he must scan the pictures in the paper to see if any of his customers have achieved athletic immortality.

Back in the Hopkinton town square, runners enter a bullpen, a snow-fence-lined area designed to protect them from autograph seekers, dogs, small children and voracious females. They mill around like happy cattle. Some already stand in their shorts, having sent their sweat suits packing by truck to the Hotel Lenox. Ten minutes before the start, officials check the runners out of the bullpen. Then they trot down the street and stand chattering in the middle of the highway. At noon the starting gun sounds.

The early pace is easy, almost luxurious compared to the slapdash start of a mile run indoors. A few morning stars flash briefly to the front, aware perhaps that photographers take pictures at two points in a race: at the start and at the finish. At the time of the finish they will be wobbling along somewhere in the vicinity of Boston College, which isn't even within spyglass range, so they might as well get their pictures in the paper at the start. Photographers and reporters sit on the back of a flatbed truck traveling just before the lead runners, their pencils poised, shutters cocked, looking for a grimace of pain, the attack of a dog, a murmur of sympathy from the crowd, so it can be dutifully reported to 500,000 Boston readers.

The marathoners flow downhill out of Hopkinton in an antlike pack, slowly stretching apart as mile piles on mile like a gob of salt-water taffy at the seashore. As early as the mile mark, hopeful little boys stand by the roadside offering orange slices to the runners. "Gee, if only Johnny Kelley would eat my orange" they think, referring to the two-time Olympian, no relation to Old John, who graduated from Boston University and won the race in 1957. But it is too early for the lead runners to think of refreshment. A couple of plodders in the rear of the pack accept slices, thus making the boys' day a success. It is easy to imagine the Boston kids' conversations the day after the great marathon as they check the results in the paper:

"Hey, the guy who took my orange finished 26th."

"So who's bragging? I got seventh place!"

Refreshments in the form of water, juice, fruit slices and wet sponges are given regularly at the various checkpoints along the 26-mile route. The rate of consumption increases in direct proportion to the temperature. Nobody ever saw Jim Beatty take a sip of water on the way to a 3:58 mile, but some replenishment of liquids seems to be necessary in a race of two and a half or more hours duration. Once while running in a 19-mile race sponsored by a veterans' post in Hamilton, Ont., I strode past a refreshment stand followed closely by several other runners. One grabbed for a cup poised on the edge of the stand. "Hey, bring that back!" fumed an official at the runner plodding away, cup in hand. The runner discovered the reason for the official's concern when he sipped from the cup. It was filled with straight whiskey.

By the first five-mile checkpoint in Framingham, a dozen runners may still share the lead. You cannot declare a leader, although the pasty blue uniforms of the two Finnish runners are usually well in evidence along with the unicorn-head insignia of the BAA worn by, among others, young John Kelley. "Go, John," yells the crowds, hopeful that he can stem the Finnish tide. Many members of the Finnish-American club that each year sponsors the expenses of the two athletes from Finland shout encouragement in their Finno-Ugric tongue. Japan has not sent a marathon team since 1959, but when it did, someone always seemed to be vaulting out of the crowd to wave a huge red-spot flag, which, considering the size of the Japanese, was usually big enough to cover both him and the runner. By the midway point a Wellesley College group of

Bermuda-shorts-clad girls, standing, like Rhine River maidens by the side of the road, cheer the runners past. They seem to be willing to applaud anyone who is male.

Several miles beyond Wellesley, the Newton Hills begin, a series of reasonably short and relatively gentle slopes that nevertheless assume Everestian proportions when taken after an hour and a half of stiff running. The crowds have thickened by this point and the runners have thinned. "Go, Higdon," they cheer. At first you think they have waited to cheer for you alone, then you realize they have simply matched your number with the list of entries in the morning paper. One year when I perhaps imprudently stayed with Kelley, the Finns, and the Japs well past the midway point, I kept hearing the comment: "Hey, who's that guy?" Some spectators note my University of Chicago Track Club running shirt and ask: "How are things in Chicago?" or "How's your football team?" I do not answer nor does the crowd expect me to. By this point my eyes resemble those of Little Orphan Annie. A small number hurl insults. "Hey, you must be nuts," I was told last year by three college types standing near the 20-mile mark. It was cold and wet. I glanced briefly at them standing there in the drizzle minus even an umbrella to protect their (pointed) heads and decided I wasn't the only one. At least I was running to get out of the rain. Most people, however, are encouraging: "The last five miles are all downhill," they chant, describing the course's topography with some accuracy. However, they have never tried to run it. The last five miles of any marathon race always feel uphill.

In the last few miles of the marathon course along Commonwealth Avenue, the watching mob thickens to three-, four-and five-deep, restrained only by their Boston manners, a rope and policemen. Individual faces in the crowd have long since disappeared from the sight of the runner. His mind focuses only on a thin yellow line in front of the Hotel Lenox.

Maybe he can sprint and overtake the runner immediately before him. But then, having trailed to this point, perhaps it would be rather impolite — and not worth the additional agony. All marathon runners are companions in pain. They do not elbow each other like milers on an indoor track. They do not attempt to outguess each other like sprinters waiting for the gun. They do not try to "psych" each other like high jumpers who skip the next height hoping to shatter the nerves of their opponents. Few races are won in the last 385 yards. It is done in the 26 miles leading up to this last insulting piece of distance — and the hundreds and thousands of miles in practice before that.

Suddenly the course bends abruptly right onto Exeter Street, and the blur of a finish line looms into view only a few hundred yards ahead. If you finish first the mayor of Boston will affectionately ring your head with a symbolic crown of thorns in the form of a laurel wreath. In Turku, Finland I once saw one such mayor crown a marathon winner with a wreath that would have seemed more in place on the doors of St. Patrick's Cathedral in New York. And he did it 100 yards before the finish line. I would have collapsed, my only request being to be carried to the nearest sauna bath. Most runners in the Boston Marathon are allowed to swoon pleasantly into the warming confines of a G.I. Army blanket, in which shroud they are whisked to the second floor of the Hotel Lenox to ease their pains in comparative privacy.

"Why do you run marathons?" echoes the query.

"Because it feels so good when I stop," screams back the now obvious answer.

If you have finished in the upper places, someone will come by the cot on which you are reclining and maybe lay a medal across your chest; a tulip would be more appropriate. After showering and having their blisters lanced by the presiding surgeon, the Boston marathoners descend to a dining room for a delicious supper of Irish stew and all the milk and soft drinks they can drink. In terms of effort required to earn it, this may be the most expensive meal in the country. But it is something that each year several hundred runners — some good, some bad, some awful — always seem willing to strive for. At 6 and 7 o'clock that evening, long, long after the noontime starting hour, you can lean out a window of the Hotel Lenox and still see an occasional runner plodding or walking along Exeter Street determined to go the entire length of the 26-mile 385-yard course. By now no one will catch him in a blanket. The officials and spectators have long since gone home, and even the dogs don't seem interested to give chase.

Last year at this late hour I exited from the hotel with a Canadian friend who had been forced out at 20 miles because of a leg injury. He was a good runner, a member of his country's Olympic team, and he had finished in the top 10 in Boston more often than not. We watched one of the late plodders stumble past the deserted finish line. "Look, Gordon," I prodded. "There's another runner finishing in front of you." I could get away with it, because in two previous attempts at running the Boston Marathon, despite some rather impressive track credentials, I had failed to finish myself after running much of the race near the lead. He mumbled something unprintable, but deep in his heart he knew I was right. In the Boston Marathon there are many victors, and not all of them cross the finish line in first place.

Hal Higdon is a contributing editor for Runner's World *and an author of three dozen books, the latest an eBook about the 2013 Boston Marathon, titled: 4:09:43. For more, visit www.halhigdon.com. This piece originally appeared in* Sports Illustrated *in 1963.*

I Don't Run Boston

by Caryl Haddock

I volunteer. There's one of us for every three or four runners. Volunteers work the expo, the starting area in Hopkinton, the entire race course, and the finish zone in Boston. That's where I work; if you're a runner, I'm one of the people handing you back your warm-up clothes, wallet, cell phone, and other impedimenta that you stashed before the race.

Some of us show up early to hand out jackets, credentials, and lunches to other volunteers well before the race even begins. When the buses arrive from Hopkinton, clothing return volunteers organize the bags with your belongings so we're ready to hand them to you when you finish. First you trickle in, but soon you start arriving in waves upon waves, and some of us scramble from bus to bus, trying to keep up with wherever the most runners are waiting. The day somehow flies by, maybe because every runner I see wearing a medal gives me a little boost of energy.

If you run Boston, I may be the last BAA volunteer you see, handing you a drawstring bag of your stuff out the window of a school bus. Then again, you may not see any more of me than my arm and hand, clutching the bag with your bib number on it, sticking out the bus window.

But I see you, runners all different heights and shapes and sizes, young and old and in between, from my own neighborhood and from all over the world. Some of you look ecstatic, some exhausted. I see that you've challenged and trained and pushed yourselves, maybe further than you ever believed you could. Maybe it's your first marathon; maybe it's your 50th, but I can see that it's still not easy, and it's always a big deal when you finish.

You're wearing shorts and capris, bun-huggers and long pants, chicken hats and tutus, technical shirts and T-shirts with pictures of people you love, and you want the rest of your clothes back so you can get dressed and find your friends and family and finally, finally, go sit down.

But there are tens of thousands of you and 55 buses full of your stuff, in thousands upon thousands of bags that shift and slide on the drive from Hopkinton to Boston, so the first thing clothing return volunteers do when the buses arrive is board them and start organizing. If it's a warm day there's not much in each bag, so it's not too hard to line them up in numerical order on the bus seats and floors and find yours quickly when you finish. If it's chilly, though, the bags are stuffed with pants and jackets (and I swear someone actually brought a blanket), and the bulging bags have to be stacked three or four deep on the seats and the floor, jammed into what little space there is between the seats, and I might have to excavate yours from the bottom. It can take a while; it probably feels like an eternity when all you want to do is get off your swelling feet.

I only started volunteering 2 years ago, but I've learned a few things. I've learned to make sure my cell phone is fully charged, because sometimes the only way to find your bag is to let you call your own cell phone and then follow the sound when it rings. Or the simplest way to help you find your friends is to lend you my phone to call them. I've learned to load subway fare on a couple of spare Charlie cards in case your bag goes astray, and you just need subway fare back to your hotel. I've learned to keep an eye peeled, especially in hot years, in case you look confused or start to sag, and make sure you get to the medical tent so other volunteers can cool you down or rehydrate you.

I've learned that you're grateful for what the volunteers do—you thank me, sometimes not because I've done anything for you personally but just because I'm wearing a volunteer's jacket. I've learned from you to thank the volunteers at the small 5Ks that I enter, because I know now how much they appreciate it.

Yes, I'm a runner too, though I don't run Boston; I volunteer. I'll be in the finish zone next year, and I hope to see you there too. Look for me; I'll be the one with my arm sticking out a school bus window.

Caryl Haddock is a medical writer who specializes in translating complex health and medical information into plain English for patients and consumers. She is also a low-mileage runner who participates in Boston's annual "Run for the Whisper" 5K to raise funds for the National Ovarian Cancer Coalition. For more, contact Caryl at fat.fish.communications@gmail.com.

(photo: courtesy MAB Community Services)

Shared Vision

by Ray Charbonneau

On April 15, I ran the 2013 Boston Marathon. It was my 22nd marathon and my fifth Boston, but this time I didn't have a number. Instead, I ran with this race bib pinned front and back:

as the sighted guide for visually impaired runner Mike Marino from Texas. We were running as part of Team With A Vision (TWAV), a group of visually impaired runners, guides, and fundraisers supporting the Massachusetts Association for the Blind and Visually Impaired (MAB).

Last fall, I was looking for something different to try after the 2012 Cape Cod Marathon, so I got in touch with Josh Warren at MAB, who added me to his list of potential runners.

Visually impaired runners can qualify for Boston by running another marathon in under 5 hours. MAB likes to match runners with guides who are at least 15 minutes faster, to make it easier for the guides to help their runners while still finishing the marathon (never an easy task). I've never dropped out of a marathon, but I have watched many people pass me by while I trudged to the finish. To keep the risk of a death-march to a minimum, I was hoping for a larger cushion. I ran a 3:25 at Cape Cod, but I figured I'd be comfortable enough guiding someone whose goal was over 4 hours.

The new year came and went. I was beginning to wonder whether MAB would need me. I kept doing my long runs so I'd be ready for a marathon if needed, though I backed off on the distances and eliminated anything resembling speedwork to keep from overtraining.

Then Mike qualified for Boston at the Houston Marathon by running a 4:38, and Josh matched us to run on Patriots Day. We exchanged contact information, and I gave Mike a call for some guidance on guiding. He explained how we would run tethered together, using a short piece of rope to signal each other. We also discussed his vision impairment, a condition called retinitis pigmentosa. He can see a little bit but only in a narrow window directly ahead, and the clarity of what he can see isn't very good.

Mike had been forced to cut back his training before Houston because of an injury. He thought he was capable of a 4:15 at Boston. He also mentioned he was going to run another marathon before Boston, The Woodlands Marathon in his hometown in Texas. I recommended that he take it easy and use Woodlands as just another long training run.

When I checked in with Mike in early March, after The Woodlands, I was surprised—and a little frightened—to find out he ran a 3:55, a 43-minute PR. That made my job a bit more interesting. He told me his new goal at Boston was 4 hours, which would be a little slower, but the Boston course is a little harder than Houston's.

I was already concerned enough about the usual things that had scuttled earlier marathons: leg cramps, dehydration, pulled muscles, and the like. On top of that, Mike is 6' 2" tall, 6 inches taller than I am, so our strides were unlikely to mesh. Toss in the fact that I'd never guided before, and I already had plenty to worry about.

A 4:15 was close to my comfortable training pace, though running 26.2 miles is hard at any speed. Sub-4? Doable, but my risk of a problem before the finish was significantly higher. I would have to spend more time focusing on my own running and less time paying attention to guiding Mike through the crowds on the course.

I've had plenty of bad marathons before. A number of times I've had to slow to a jog or even walk to keep going. I've never had to drop out of a marathon, but there's a first time for everything. That's okay if it's my race—but this was Mike's race. I was there to help him. If I had any problems that kept Mike from achieving his goal, it would take me a while to forgive myself.

Since Mike lives in Texas, we couldn't get together for any practice before Boston Marathon weekend. Mike wasn't worried. He told me we'd figure out what we were doing in the first couple of miles and go from there. Still, when I suggested that we get together the day before the race to jog together a little bit, he agreed that it would be a good idea.

By this point, with less than a month to go before Boston, there wasn't a whole lot I could do to prepare for a faster race. I did a few weeks of hill repeats, wrapped up my final long runs, including a 20-miler with some of the other TWAV runners, and then it was time to taper for the marathon.

I checked in with Mike again during race week. He told me that after some additional thought, he'd decided that 4:15 would be a more reasonable goal in a hilly race like Boston. I let out a sigh of relief, and then suggested we go out at that pace, run through the Newton hills, and then, if he still felt comfortable, we could take advantage of the relatively easy terrain over the last few miles to push it in.

Sunday, the morning before the race, Mike and I finally met in person. MAB had found him a place to stay at the Carroll Center for the Blind in Newton. We met there and jogged around the parking lot for a few minutes, tethered together with a necktie provided by Josh, since Mike had forgotten to pack a rope. It wasn't much practice, but at least I proved that I wouldn't seriously damage Mike right away.

After our little jog we went inside the Carroll Center, where I met some of the other runners and their guides. Then a MAB van brought us to the Westin Copley in Boston for the MAB Volunteer Appreciation Brunch, where we picked up our TWAV uniforms and met some of the people who help MAB provide their services.

After the brunch, Mike and I walked with some of the other runners over to the marathon expo to pick up our race numbers. Mike needed me to give directions, but he had no problem making his way through the crowded sidewalks to the Hynes Auditorium.

Inside the Hynes, the halls were filled with people rushing to find their number or the room where their favorite runner was speaking. We picked up our bibs and goodie bags, then we went into the main hall, where the congestion was worse. People were packed elbow to elbow, struggling their way from one booth to another to shop for gear. We found it worked better to have Mike lead me through the crowds, carrying his cane in front of him, while I gave directions as necessary from behind. As he put it, "People make way for the blind guy."

The next morning, I was back at the Westin Copley bright and early to catch one of vans taking TWAV members out to the Hopkinton Vision Center, where we would wait for the race to begin. The Vision Center was a little crowded, but that just made it easier to meet the rest of the team. TWAV also provided snacks and drinks. Before Boston, I'm usually sitting on a bus or pacing around in a field. It was an entirely new experience for me to be treated like an elite runner, with a place to wait in a comfortable office located a block away from the start. I could get used to it.

Mike and I were in the third wave, so we didn't start until 10:40 a.m. I tend to be a little tense before races—doubly so when it's a big event like Boston. Mike, however, was just as calm as he had been the day before, though he admitted to a little impatience with the late start.

Finally, the time came to head out to the starting corrals for the race. It was a short walk out to Main Street in Hopkinton, where Mike and I crowded into our corral along with thousands of other runners. The gun went off and the teeming masses slowly moved forward. After a couple minutes of walking, Mike and I made it to the timing mat at the start, I pressed the button on my GPS watch, and we were off.

While slowly picking our way through the thickest crowds of the race, we worked out how we would run together. I quickly realized that the tether worked better if I took up some of the slack. I ended up running side-by-side with Mike with less than a foot between us. We frequently bumped arms, but that helped us keep track of each other's location. Our heights and our strides were quite different. That forced us to cut back the natural swing of our tethered arms, so Mike had us switch sides every 5 miles to even out the strain.

After the first mile, the runners started to spread out, which let us speed up. I was using my GPS to measure split times for us. Mike was turning in sub-9 minute miles, well under the 9:40s he'd need to finish at 4:15. I'd read the splits to him and ask him how he felt about going that fast. He was okay with it. I didn't want to discourage Mike if he wanted to run faster, so I decided to just go along for the ride, keep track, and see if maybe we could end up running a sub-4 after all.

Since Mike was seeded in his corral according to his 4:38 at Houston, we were faster than most of the runners we started with. That helped us keep some control over how we interacted with the runners around us, though it meant that we spent a lot of time weaving through packs of slower runners.

Obviously, most of the time I was the one deciding where we were going to go. I was constantly scanning the runners ahead of us, looking for spaces wide enough for two people to fit through. When I saw something, I'd call out the direction and either tug on the necktie or give Mike's arm a nudge to provide a little additional information. When we were lined up properly, with the opening in Mike's field of vision, I'd say okay, give the opposite signal to stop our sideways motion, and then we'd move through the gap.

My other role was to warn Mike about obstacles in the road. Luckily the course between Hopkinton and Boston is in pretty good shape. I had to warn him about chip mats and railroad tracks, but there were only a few places where I had to point out a rough surface. That was good, because I was kept busy enough watching out for other runners.

We got better at it as we went along, until it became almost automatic. As we got more comfortable, we got a little more aggressive. Sometimes Mike would see a gap ahead of him and go for it, but since his field of vision was narrow, he wouldn't realize that it wasn't quite wide enough for the two of us. There were a few times I had to hold him back, but for the most part I could just fall into line behind him until we made it through and then accelerate for a second to get back to his side.

Once I realized Mike wanted to go for it, I started leading him through those gaps, darting into his field of vision and calling, "Follow me!" We'd shoot through, I'd slow down for a few steps so he could get back to my side, and then I'd start looking for the next gap. Every once in a while, we'd pull into a spot where there was space ahead of us to run without weaving from side to side — but that didn't happen very often, or last for very long. We certainly weren't running the tangents.

We side-swiped a few people, but not many more than I would have if I were running by myself through the crowds. Mike only had two significant collisions, both early in the race when runners directly ahead of us decided to stop suddenly. The first person was just oblivious (and wearing headphones), while the second stopped to pick up a sweatband that another runner had discarded. In both cases, Mike let me know he was okay, and we got back on track right away.

Sweatbands were necessary. It was a warm spring day, with the temperature rising as the day went on. By the middle of the race, the weather was the warmest I'd run in yet this year. Even Mike, used to the warmer weather in Texas, started to get a little too hot as we ran through Wellesley. I was sweating profusely, and I had to throw water in my face at one of the stops in order to rinse the salt out of my eyes.

All the watching and steering kept me busy enough so the miles seemed to fly by. Meanwhile Mike, even with his limited sight, was enjoying the pageantry of the race while we ran. Afterward, he told me some of the things that stood out: a guy with bunny ears, passing a three-and-a-half-foot-tall woman, an amputee running with a blade leg, and the woman who stopped in front of him to puke. Still, his main focus was on his race. When I asked him if he wanted to run through the crowd in front of the Wellesley women, he chose to bypass the screaming wall, and we sped by on the other side of the road.

Luckily, a cool sea breeze began to blow in our faces, providing some relief as we approached the firehouse turn in Newton. Thousands of marathons have foundered there, in the series of four hills between miles 17 and 21. All of Mike's previous marathons have been on flat courses, so the hills were a big challenge for him. He was ready for them. Our pace slowed and we lost some ground towards a sub-4 finish, but Mike kept running and we kept passing people as we climbed each hill.

Just after we passed the chip mat at the 30K mark, there was an enormous roar to our left, with dozens of people leaning out onto the course and screaming, "Go Mike!" Mike was baffled, figuring that everybody was cheering for some other Mike, until I explained it to him. My running club, the Somerville Road Runners, had a tent there. I had asked my friends in SRR to cheer for Mike, not me, when they saw us, and they did me proud.

After that, we passed the Johnny Kelley statue and climbed the third hill. When we reached the top, I told Mike that the worst of it was over. Then we hit Heartbreak, which looked to Mike, "like a wall of people on a giant escalator." Halfway up, he was struggling, but he had enough breath to complain that I'd said this would be "just a bump." I cheerfully admitted that I might have lied.

That was Mike's slowest mile of the race. But once we crested Heartbreak, Mike recovered quickly and sped right up again. When he saw some space, he'd jump ahead, forcing me to accelerate to catch up. By this time I was starting to get tired. Each time I had to break into a run to chase Mike down, I was wondering in the back of my mind if I'd be able to do it. But I answered the call every time. And even though running faster was harder, once I caught up it was pleasant to cruise along for a minute or two at something more like my normal pace.

As we zoomed along, we caught up with a slower woman runner so quickly that I didn't have time to decide whether to go to the left or to the right. Instead, I shouted, "Up!" By this time we were working so well together that we both instantly raised our arms, split, and went around her on either side, our arms still connected by the necktie passing cleanly over her head. As Mike noted later, it was a good thing she was short.

While we ran, I was looking at my watch and furiously doing math in my head, trying to figure out how we were doing. The race clocks were no help because I wasn't sure how much time we had lost at the start. We were at mile 24 when I realized that if we could finish strong, we might just sneak in at under 4 hours. I shared that with Mike, and he was up for the attempt.

In the last 2 miles, there were finally some extended stretches where we could run along the edge of the road without having to weave through people. Mike took full advantage, and we finished mile 26 in 8:36, our second-fastest split of the day.

When we turned right on Hereford, left on Boylston, and Mike sensed the banners at the finish, he found a clear path down the middle of the road and charged for the line. According to my GPS, he hit a 6:38 pace during this last sprint. Unfortunately, the reason there was a clear path was that most runners went to one side or the other, to avoid a large group of cameramen in the center of the road, just past the finish. Mike crashed through the cameras—somehow without incident—with me running alongside, struggling to keep up.

We finished with the clock reading 4:02:15. Mike's chip time of 3:58:47 placed him 11th in the Visually Impaired division. This graph shows how Mike's splits compare to the splits for a nominal "even effort" runner:

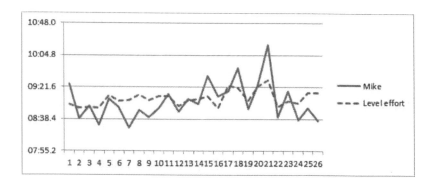

We all know what happened at about 4:09 on the clock, just after we received our finisher's medals. I'm not going into that here. Instead, I'm taking Mike's advice and focusing on the good things that happened—and there were plenty of those.

I had an amazing time. I've helped plenty of people get through marathons before—with advice, by sharing training runs, or by providing support on the side of the road during a race—but nothing like this. I'm grateful to Team With A Vision, and especially to Mike, for the opportunity.

I'll leave it to Mike to wrap this up. After all, it was his race. I was just there to read the map along the way.

My Boston marathon experience was more than just the race. As a blind person, I find that sighted people always have trouble relating to what it is like to lose vision and how to live life with a positive outlook. Being surrounded by blind and VI athletes from around the country was an amazingly therapeutic experience for me. They're a courageous group of people. It was great to hear how others deal with the loss of vision and that, although life can be frustrating at times, it can be very fulfilling. We also exchanged tricks of the trade.

I also found the guides to be very gracious. Most were amazing athletes who have accomplished goals in running most people can only dream of. They all had a common thread in that running wasn't just about achieving personal goals, but a vehicle to be a part of something bigger then themselves.

Being guided is an exercise in placing faith in someone else's hand. Over all, that has been the greatest gift of going blind—it keeps the ego in check and adds a huge dose of humility. I am able to see people's true kindness more than others.

As for the race itself, the Boston Marathon is like none other—I see why it's like Wimbledon is to tennis or the Masters is to golf. The historic course was challenging, the crowds were uplifting, and the other runners were amazing.

Over all, the race was a memorable experience that I will treasure always. Some people may focus on the tragedy at the race. My fellow blind and VI athletes don't focus on the tragedy of vision loss. Instead, we dig deep into the human spirit and turn that tragedy into a beautiful thing. I know the spirit of Boston will do the same.

Ray Charbonneau has run well over 200 races. It doesn't bother him (much) that he lost every single one of them. Ray is the author of Overthinking the Marathon, Chasing the Runner's High, *and* R is for Running. *For more, visit y42k.com. "Shared Vision" is an original piece for* The 27th Mile.

Do We Need an Ambulance for Cross Country?

by Grace Butcher

> "Do We Need an Ambulance for Cross Country?"
> *Question from the audience*
> *at a sports medicine seminar*
> *for coaches.*

And the scene comes unbidden into my mind:
the runners at the farthest turn of the course,
behind the roughest field and into the woods,
among the deepest trees left leaning
after last year's storm.

The alien colors trickle down the path:
the red & black, the purple & gold, the green & white.
We strain to see the brilliant flashes
through the dying leaves, but must wait,
murmuring to ourselves, "Where are they?
Where are they?"

I know where they are. I sent them there.
I know every stone, every rut and hole,
every root waiting to trap the delicate foot,
the feet of my slender animals,
claws scratching the dirt, striking sparks
from the flat rock on that sharp turn.
And I see one try to pass,
try to take the lead,
see the root reach for him
with a thin gray arching arm
that will not let go.

169

I hear the snap of something else,
the scream drift down the hill
through the golden leaves,
feel my face go white with fear.

I sent him there, sent all of them.
They go for glory
and because I told them to,
knowing all the while
how fragile the bones,
how fixed ahead the eyes are,
forgetting to look down, forgetting
in the beauty of the run
that anything can end in a second,
even when you are young
and protected by the names of fierce animals.

I hear the answer. It is yes.
My head swims. The auditorium
is too hot. I leave abruptly,
walk into the cool darkness,
look up, find the first star,
make my wish.

Grace Butcher started competing in 1949, winning the Cleveland Junior Olympic hurdles championship and multiple national championships in the 880/800. Her most recent title was Masters National Indoor 400 champion at Boston in 2003. Grace has published five books of poetry (she was the Ohio Poet of the Year in 1992) and a collection of columns from Rider *magazine on motorcycling. She taught English at Kent State (Geauga Campus) for 25 years, founded their running program and coached it for 12 years. Grace put competing on hold when she went back to her earliest passion, riding and training horses, but she continues running for fitness and sanity, and she plans to win the Masters Worlds 800 in the 120 - 124 age group when that comes along. "Do We Need an Ambulance for Cross Country?" was first published in* Aethlon: The Journal of Sport Literature.

Awakenings and Resolutions

by Kathrine Switzer

"No, it wasn't a surprise to me. At all."

That was what I answered to the first question almost all the journalists asked in the immediate aftermath of the bombings that took place on the finish line of the Boston Marathon on April 15. In fact, I wanted to add that this monster has been lurking in my mind for years, and now that it is out at last, we can talk about it.

Mentioning it publicly before could have put the thought in some psychotic's head. We've been awakened. Now perhaps we can find resolution.

Terrorism has no reason or excuse. But it does love a photo op.

My monster first crept out of envelopes after I ran the Boston Marathon in 1967. After a race official attacked me for running in what was then a race for men only, I received a lot of mail. Most of it was "You go, girl!" fan mail, but several letters from weirdos were quite menacing.

As the women's movement in general became more assertive, and more of us were pushing for inclusion in all areas, it seemed that women in the Boston Marathon were particularly confrontational. And visible. In gun-happy America, I was aware that a wild-eyed sniper could easily take one of us out as we came down Boylston Street to the finish. This I could understand, because it was personal. Fortunately, running makes you fearless. Besides, we had a job to do.

At the 1972 Munich Olympics, Palestinian terrorists known as al Fatah sneaked into the Olympic Village and murdered 12 Israeli team members. As a 25-year-old sports journalist in Munich to cover the track and field, I'd never even heard of al Fatah. I could not grasp why anyone would commit such an act, and was shattered that they would do it on the holy altar of the Olympics. How naïve could I have been? As if terrorists have a conscience! While I didn't quite become a cynic after this, I was never surprised again, and neither should any of us be.

We've worked years to make our geeky innocent marathons big and glamorous. Now they have grown to be so mainstream and prosperous that they have changed the face of our major cities. So we should not be surprised that these populated, joyful events have also provided an irresistible Media Moment for the bombers. If it wasn't Boston, it was going to be London, Berlin, Chicago, or New York. Especially New York. For me, anyway.

The New York City Marathon 2001 was the first time I was truly terrified. Not surprised, but terrified. My husband, Roger Robinson, and I lived in heart of New York City and were there for 9/11. Only seven weeks after those terrorist attacks, while the smoke was still rising from the rubble of the World Trade Center, the decision was made to go forward with the New York City Marathon. I must confess I had a heavy heart, because I'd long had dark thoughts that blowing up the Verrazano Narrows Bridge, with 25,000 runners on it, would be a spectacular terrorist opportunity—even more, perhaps, than flying planes into the twin towers. You have morbid thoughts like this when you are on a motorcycle sidecar doing the TV commentary at the lead of the women's race, because you know you'll be the first to go. But running also makes you resolute, and besides, I had a job to do. Still, Roger says that one of his moments of greatest relief was seeing my motorcycle swoop safely off the bridge.

It was a surrealistic scene at the New York City Marathon that year. Extra early road closures, metal detectors, bag searches for all of the runners and volunteers, snipers in flak suits on the rooftops, frogmen checking the underwater bridge

174

pilings for bombs. The finish line area, normally crammed with screaming spectators and overloaded bleachers, was strangely sparse and quiet, because you couldn't get in without very strict credentials. It's worth remembering this scene, because it may be the future look of the marathon running experience for all of us.

It was slightly surrealistic at 8:00 a.m. on the brisk sunny morning of April 15, when I walked the 100 or so yards from the media center at the Fairmont Copley Plaza Hotel to our WBZ-TV position on the photo bridge at the finish line of the Boston Marathon. I'd made this trip for 44 years, 8 as a runner and 36 as a TV commentator. Policemen with three sniffer dogs were doing a back-and-forth sweep of the entire finish line area, and I thought, "Gee, it's too bad on such a beautiful, joyful day, we need to worry about security." But I was glad they were there.

In fact the whole week had been joyful. In the days before, local media were all a-twitter over the glamorous Shalane Flanagan–Kara Goucher duo and the real possibility that they could be the first American women winners since 1985. At the same time, thousands of runners from all over the world mugged for their cell phone photos at the finish line, they jammed the seminars, they waited in long lines at expos for autographs from their favorite runners, and they bought everything in sight with a big "Who cares?" smile over their diminishing credit card limit. It's the Boston Marathon, after all—a once in a lifetime experience.

Among hundreds of others, I hugged Kathy Voigtschild, a 3:29 woman who hoped to run close to her 3:40 qualifying time. Kathy has five kids aged 10 and under, including three-year-old triplets. (How in the world do you have time to train and qualify for the Boston Marathon when you have three-year-old triplets?!) Then there were two sisters from Saudi Arabia who kept saying, "We escaped and now we want to be athletes!" Most of the runners were like my girlfriends Rhonda Provost and Rosemary Spraker, who qualified for Boston but were not at their best and were planning on running "about four hours." Then there were friends Les Potapcyck, Bob Kaminsky, and Jimmy Moran, race directors who annually travel to Boston from their own events to volunteer at finish line crowd control. We all had jobs to do and were out there joyfully doing them.

I climbed up the ladder of the photo bridge, made my usual joke about hoping the station had a good insurance policy (this bridge always feels rickety and dangerous loaded with TV equipment), and joined my colleagues Toni Reavis and anchor Lisa Hughes. We did a five-hour telecast, and unique this year was the 26 seconds of pre-race silence devoted to the 26 little children and their teachers from nearby Sandy Hook, Connecticut, who were killed last December by a deranged gunman. All of New England was deeply affected by this atrocity, and so, for the first time in 117 years, the Boston Marathon was started with an air horn, not with a gun, as a symbol of anti-violence feelings. When our show was over, Toni and I walked back to the hotel. Lisa said she'd see us later at the awards ceremony. She would wait a while for a friend to finish the race.

After signing in with Roger, who was completing his article in the pressroom, I went up to our room. Almost immediately, the first blast of a bomb went off. I thought the window of our hotel room was going to burst in. Then, the second explosion. The street below, filled with the sparkle of foil blankets, the clinking of finishers' medals, the color and laughter of friends and relatives, turned quickly into a deserted kind of moonscape as police moved confused and distressed people out, and police cars, ambulances, and then very sinister-looking black vans raced in. Everything, our hotel included, went into lockdown. In just a moment, the only sound was wailing sirens. Roger walked in the door. We fell into each other's arms. We were so, so lucky. Some totally innocent people lost their arms. Their legs. Their lives.

My story, filled with ironies and sadness, is not unique. I tell mine only as an example. Everyone who was at Boston that day and walked away has a dramatic story, and all of them include the near-misses, the what-ifs, but more achingly, the sheer panic of not knowing the fate of someone you care about and the utter desolation of being unable to tell those you love where you are. I wanted desperately to call my mother. My mother has been dead for over 10 years.

It's impossible to grasp and sort it all. With a pounding heart, I turned on the TV station I work for, and saw the video of the blast, noting that the finish line clock was at 4:09. Then I saw Lisa Hughes, and relieved tears sprang into my eyes. She was still on the photo bridge, bravely but with a quivering voice doing commentary from her cell phone. The incredulity and relief of her being there — of the bridge still being there — is mixed with the horror of what she had to be seeing as she looked down on the scene.

You try to convince yourself that your friends are OK. Kathy must have run her 3:40. But on a bad day that could easily be four hours, and what about her husband and the five kids waiting on the finish line? Herding five kids takes a long time… .

Rhonda and Rosemary always run what they say they'll run. "About" four hours will be either four hours, or 4:15 … or maybe 4:09. Maybe, just maybe, they've missed it… .

But Les, Jimmy, and Bob — for sure they are RIGHT THERE, alongside the barriers. Their job is to stay until the end.

Within a few hours, we found out that all of our friends were safe — a miraculously lucky coincidence of timing. Lisa, Les, Jimmy, and Bob rose to heroic status by continuing their duties in the face of great danger. Indeed, they were shining examples of the volunteers and medical people on hand at the finish who saved many lives. Injured people got help in time because they were there.

The police were extraordinary. Luckily, hundreds of them were already on site and could go into action immediately. They had done their job with the sniffer dogs in the morning, but the bombers dropped their bags in the crowd later in the day, probably aware of that fact. The follow-up police work was exceptional, including turning to the public for help with video identification and locking down the entire city of Boston. The bombers were apprehended within one of the most amazing weeks of which any of us have ever been a part.

We have had an awakening. Now, in its immediate aftermath, can we find any resolution?

Within an hour, London Marathon officials issued upgraded security reports for their following weekend's race. Race directors all over the world began meeting with local police to re-secure their events. The reality is that you cannot secure 26.2 miles of public roads, and everyone understands that the joy and purpose of a marathon is to run from one point to another. Yet start and finish areas—the media hot spots—will be more controlled in the future. Some joyful spontaneity may be lost, but it is a small price to pay.

At the Christie Clinic Illinois Marathon on April 27, the biggest marathon in the USA immediately post-Boston, the race directors and local police were under enormous pressure, and yet not a bit of exuberance was lost. On the contrary, crowds were bigger than ever, and the start and stadium finish were full of excitement, with no sense of restriction. Police and sniffer dogs were clearly there, but they moved amiably throughout the crowd. In London, every runner wore a black ribbon in tribute to Boston, and officials were stunned by the great increase in spectators along the course, many of whom dressed in Boston colors or held Boston tribute signs. In races all over the world, emotion has been at an all-time high.

From the bombers, we still want to know: Why? To this, sadly, we will never have resolution. Terrorism has no valid reason, no excuse, and no conscience. That is why, in spite of what we see on the daily news, many were still surprised by what occurred on Boylston St. It was a painful lesson, but we won't be surprised again.

The determination, generosity, and solidarity of runners after this terrible awakening are an inspiring example to the rest of the world. Running is about freedom, and from its first inception, the marathon was about that freedom, about resolve, and fearlessness. In one of the many (seemingly endless) interviews that we did on the afternoon of the bombing, I said, "If the Boston Marathon were held tomorrow, a million people would want to run it." And when it is held next year, two million people will want to run it. Right now, this is our resolution.

Kathrine Switzer changed the running world in 1967 by becoming the first woman to run the Boston Marathon with an official number, in spite of an attempt by co-director Jock Semple to pull her off the course in the midst of the race. Kathrine went on to help build a movement that led to the inclusion of the women's marathon in the Olympic Games and a global fitness and empowerment revolution for women. Switzer has run 39 marathons (PR, 2:51:37), won the 1974 New York City Marathon, and still runs marathons today, at age 66. She is also a TV commentator; the author of three books, including her memoir, Marathon Woman; *and an activist for women everywhere. This article originally appeared in* Marathon & Beyond.

Finding Resilience in the Forest

by Vanessa Runs

While some people have fond memories of themselves as children, with days full of opportunity and innocence and mornings spent chasing puppies and rainbows, my own memories are clouded with the uncomfortable sensation of a complete lack of control. It is a fear-based aura assuring you that something bad may happen at any moment, and there is absolutely nothing you can do about it.

It had been years since I'd felt that old panicky chill, like a frigid hand creeping up the back of my neck — until the day of the Boston Marathon 2013.

I was exploring a nearby creek with the dog as we boondocked outside of Zion National Park, in Utah. My boyfriend Shacky was able to pick up some 3G and checked his Facebook account. A few seconds later, he informed me that someone had detonated two bombs at the Boston Marathon finish line. We knew nothing else. My first reaction was disbelief, followed by worry for my friends who were running the race. The feeling was magnified by the fact that we didn't have a reliable wifi connection or phone service. Off the grid, we didn't know our friends were safe until a couple of days later.

After Zion, we visited Sequoia National Park. I spent the drive reading various blogs of people reacting to the bombings. I knew the feeling: that something bad could happen at any moment, and there was nothing we could do about it. It took me a long time to process the Boston events, so instead of sending my underdeveloped thoughts out into the blogosphere, I sought refuge under the towering sequoias. Many of these trees had stood for at least one thousand years and had survived the harshest conditions imaginable. What could they teach me about tragedy?

Back in the 1800s, park rangers scrambled to put out the natural forest fires they believed threatened the sequoias. Although they were successful, the rangers soon noticed something unusual: The ancient trees stopped growing.

Richard Hartesveldt took it upon himself to investigate this puzzling matter. He learned that these magnificent trees were resilient enough to survive even the most intense fires, and depended on wildfire to clear out their competition for fertile ground, a reliable water source, and sunshine. They were difficult to destroy. (If the trunk of the General Grant sequoia tree were a gas tank on a car that got 25 miles per gallon, you could drive around the earth 350 times without refueling.)

Hartesveldt's most fascinating discovery was the fact that the wildfire heat was responsible for prying open the sequoia's pinecones and releasing its seeds. Sequoia seeds would fall onto the ash residue from the fires — the ideal fertile ground for baby trees. These babies would someday soar to an average weight of 700 tons — more than two fully loaded jumbo jet planes — transforming what was once a hotspot into a deep, dense forest floor. Millions of seedlings would sprout after a single fire.

Sequoias need fire. Their nature is to take root in the midst of adversity.

Lewis L. Davis was the first civilian park ranger in the early 1900s. He moved into a cabin on the park's property and patrolled the grove for seven years, patiently raising sequoia seeds and learning more about their relationship with fire.

A century later, I ran through the forest and stopped to caress the deep burn scars at the base of the powerful trunks of trees that Davis had cared for. These trees not only overcame adversity, but used tragedy as a tool to develop a new generation of giants.

In life, there will always be fires. It's a natural reaction to panic when we smell the smoke. But as the heat starts to rise in our own lives, we should think of the sequoias. We can't always control the fire, but we can always stand resiliently among the flames as proud examples to those who will someday run there.

Vanessa Runs is an ultrarunner and author of The Summit Seeker. *This piece originally appeared on her blog, vanessaruns.com.*

Wheels

by RJ Walker

Since the invention of the wheel,
who knows how long ago,
it has been praised as the successor to walking.
The way cars carry people so far
so fast.
It is a speed I have only dreamed of.

I am jealous of the way
bicycles, skateboards, and roller skates
have made transportation so creative,
so enjoyable.

While I do have wheels,
I am not the successor to walking.
I am a backup plan.
I am a wheelchair.

I was not made for mountain paths
or half pipes.
I was made for aftermath.
I was made for those who've changed their slogan
from "Just do it"
to "Shouldn't have done that…"

The architect of my design
must have had perfect hindsight.
If I could, I would ask him
whether he intended me as a vehicle
or a prosthesis?
And why do wheelchairs have dreams of running?

I just want to be somebody's legs
instead of their last resort.
"I'm just helping them through a rough patch"
they say.
They don't know what a rough patch is.
They've never tried to push a wheelchair
through tall grass or mud.

If every staircase is a mountain,
what does that make the actual mountains?
I'd say it makes a challenge
and as long as there are challenges,
there are those who would accept them.

You know what they say:
If you fall off your horse
modify the shit out of it
and get right back on.

I wasn't made for half pipes,
but don't think that will stop me.
I am not just a prosthesis.
I am not just a vehicle.
I am both.

Capability is a substance
that is measured in motivation.
The best part about being a mechanism
is that you are only limited by physics
and imagination.

I am not a backup plan.
I am the last bastion

for those who refuse to accept their circumstances.

You think four minutes is a fast mile?
Just wait until someone decides to bolt on wings.

RJ Walker is a spoken word artist in multiple forms, including stand-up comedy and performance poetry. He is a member of the 2013 Salt City Slam poetry team. RJ works as an EMT and has provided emergency medical service at the Mud Run, the Spartan Race, and the Undie Run, as well as aquatic rescue service for two triathlons. It's mostly on a volunteer basis, but sometimes they pay him in granola and T-shirts.

Why I'll Run the Marathon in 2014

by Ray Charbonneau

For my 22nd marathon, I volunteered to guide visually-impaired runner Mike Merino in the Boston Marathon. We were part of the Massachusetts Association for the Blind's Team With A Vision. Mike and I tethered ourselves together at the start in Hopkinton and then weaved our way through crowds of runners to the finish on Boylston Street.

After I guided Mike across the line, we jammed ourselves in with hundreds of other tired, sweaty runners stumbling slowly forward to collect the medals commemorating our victory. We were a scrawny army wrapped in foil blankets. Survivors of a war we'd fought in flimsy uniforms and boots padded with lightweight foam, armed only with bodies loaded with pasta, oxygen from a beautiful spring day, and determination. The fight to finish in under four hours had taken all we had.

Then there was an explosion. While we were still trying to convince ourselves that the first blast was just an accident—maybe a short in a power transformer or a gas leak—another one went off. We knew then, though it wouldn't be confirmed until much later, that the real war had intruded, the one with bombs and flying shreds of metal and glass. The one with four tragic deaths, and more than 260 people injured, some severely.

My first response, and the first response of many of the people I know, wasn't fear. It was anger. We were mad, and are still mad, because running is our refuge, and someone was trying to take it away.

Running helps me process my thoughts. It distracts me just enough to let the back of my mind sort out whatever is bothering me. An hour's run is a straightforward task that gives me the comfort of knowing I've accomplished something that day. If I argue with my boss or get in a fight with my spouse, I can work through it by running a little faster. And a nice, long run is a few hours out of the day where I don't have to worry about yard work, bills, politics, crime, or terrorism.

At least until that Monday, when someone decided they needed to make a point of some kind at the Boston Marathon.

Non-runners have asked me whether I'll be afraid to return to the marathon next year. They don't understand: if I was afraid, running is what I'd do to work through those feelings.

But running isn't just about escaping the stresses of daily life. We don't run just to get fit, for the competition, or to collect money for charities. Those are wonderful benefits, but they're not why we run. As Mike told me on Tuesday, "I run marathons because of something bigger than all that."

It starts with individual people, getting out on the road regularly, building fitness, and training to run farther and faster. As they run, they find others who share their goals and start working together, having fun while encouraging each other to achieve even more. Some of those people organize events, and even more people, many of them non-runners, join in to help. Soon there are 24,000 people running together from Hopkinton to Boston with thousands more in volunteer jackets helping out, hundreds of thousands lining the roads to cheer and enjoy the spectacle, and millions donating to their friend's charity, watching on TV, and maybe even thinking, "Hey, I'll bet I can do that."

It's also about the next day, when the crowds are gone and you're out there by yourself, not for the glory, but because it's who you are: a runner. And it's about getting out there the next day and the next and the one after that.

Usually, distance runners toil on the side of the road, away from any spotlight other than the headlights from an oncoming car. Our sport only gets noticed in the US in passing, when the Summer Olympics are held in a convenient time zone or on the weekend of the Boston Marathon.

Now we're getting worldwide attention, but for all the wrong reasons. And it makes us mad.

Sure, lots of people were disappointed that they didn't get to finish their race, but that's not the real issue. Marathoners are used to the vagaries of the weather or a mid-race injury spoiling six months of training. It's frustrating, but there's always another race. The bombers wanted to destroy that possibility of redemption.

Marathoners already know running Boston isn't a given. Most people have to qualify by running fast or collecting for a charity. If we aren't able to earn our way in, that's OK. But we are not willing to let someone else take our opportunity away.

Angry people set off the bombs in Boston that Monday. We runners are angry too, but we're going to use that as fuel to train harder and become better runners, so when we show up in Hopkinton in 2014, we'll be ready to do our best in memory of those who fell on April 15, 2013.

Ray Charbonneau is a member of the Somerville Road Runners, Crow Athletics, the Trail Animals Running Club, the Idiots Running Club, and probably a few others. He's also the editor of The 27th Mile. *For more, visit y42k.com. "Why I'll Run the Marathon in 2014" originally appeared in* The Christian Science Monitor.

Acknowledgements

When I started this project, I told people I would be shameless about asking for help, and I was. You would not be reading this book without the assistance of the many people who came through. Here are some of them, in no particular order:

- The writers, of course. Not only did they provide the words, but many of them helped connect me with additional writers to make the book even better.
- Ryan Bradley, who designed the cover from a picture I took at the living memorial in Copley Square.
- Foxxe Editorial Services, Susan Fish at Storywell.ca, and Caryl Haddock for their help with the editing.
- Francine Kiefer at the *Christian Science Monitor*, Suzanne Perrault at *Runner's World*, Jonathan Beverly at *Running Times*, and Rich Benyo at *Marathon & Beyond* for their help in clearing rights to some of the pieces in the book.
- Heather Hagerty, Susan L. Abbott at Goodwin Procter LLP, and Ken Feinberg at The One Fund Boston for help with questions related to the fund.
- Angelo Matheou, of the Endorphin Report, for allowing the use of the the27thmile.com domain.
- Jim Brennan, for the mental image of Johnny Kelly watching over the finish line.
- Walter Powers at the MIT Libraries, my go-to cataloging expert.

And numerous other people who answered questions, provided ideas, or helped spread the word.

I'm taking advantage of my position as editor to thank some additional people:

- Josh Warren of the Massachusetts Association for the Blind and Visually Impaired, for hooking me up to run the 2013 Boston Marathon as a sighted guide.
- Mike Merino, for running Boston with me and teaching me something about trust.
- My wife, Ruth Sespaniak, for innumerable reasons, not the least of which is making it possible for me to have the time to work on this book.

And finally, and most importantly, **You**, for buying and reading this book (and telling all your friends about it). It's your money that goes to help the victims.

Hope to see you all in Hopkinton on Patriots Day!

—Ray

26780979R00105

Made in the USA
Lexington, KY
18 October 2013